To Donna,
Thanks for coming on an
eastbound cruise with it.

W9-AXW-228

Reliving
Lighthouse Memories
1930s - 1970s

by Sandra L. Planisek

Sandy Planisek

with the help of
Richard L. Moehl
Terry Pepper

Great Lakes Lighthouse Keepers Association
206 Lake St.
P. O. Box 219
Mackinaw City, MI 49701
www.GLLKA.com

© 2004 by Sandra L. Planisek and the
Great Lakes Lighthouse Keepers Association,
exclusive of government photographs

All rights reserved. No part of this book may be reproduced or utilized in any form or by any electronic or mechanical means including photocopying, recording, or by any information storage and retrieval system, without permission in writing from the Great Lakes Lighthouse Keepers Association, except by a reviewer who may quote brief passages in a review.

ISBN 0-940767-06-6

Printed in U.S.A.

On the cover: Bill Simon at Martin Reef

Great Lakes Lighthouse Keepers Association
P. O. Box 219
Mackinaw City, MI 49701
231-436-5580

This book is dedicated to Dick Moehl,
who made this book, and so much more, possible.

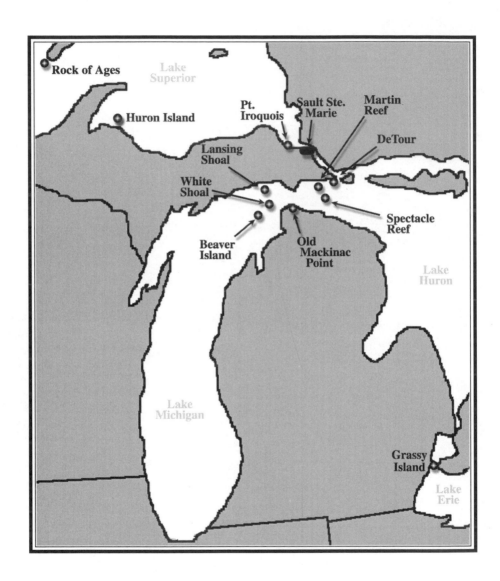

TABLE OF CONTENTS

Reading the Book

The speakers in this book have been kind enough to take us through their unique memories and share their life at lighthouses during a period when lighthouses were manned by living keepers and their families. As with all adults, memories are spotty. Only the outstanding moments are clear, but in the interview process we tried to broaden the memories to include the mundane and typical aspects of life as well.

After spending hours and hours with these people, we then had to translate the oral histories into written histories with the constant question of what to do about oral idioms that do not translate well to the written word. We did correct some grammar, simplify repetitive sentences, and in some cases, rearrange the questions and answers to clarify the reading.

We also had the problem of how to spell people's names. When feasible we checked references and used the published spellings, but some of the people in this book were not listed in references. So we spelled names phonetically as best we could, and in these cases apologize for any errors.

We have used the practice of italicizing our questions which are then followed by the answers. In a few cases we added explanations in the answers and these are enclosed in parentheses.

In an effort to keep the tone of the speakers, we did not correct affectionate names for people or lighthouses. Almost everyone used a pet name or abbreviation for the places that became home. These places were not just home, they were demanding friends that left lasting memories and emotions.

Lastly, in the artwork at the beginning of chapters and sub-chapters we have used GLLKA's logo lighthouse. This is a reminder that this book was produced by volunteers for GLLKA. The proceeds will be used to support lighthouse preservation.

The Book

The youngest person interviewed in this book was in his mid-60s, the rest were in their 70s, 80s or 90s. They have had a lot of intervening experiences to interfere with and to compare against the lighthouse memories. This book tells the actual history of lighthouses from the 1930s thru the 1970s. The stories are true, as best as the authors can remember. However, that does not guarantee that these stories are typical. Each story is the tale of that particular person's experience. Seven people, seven stories. The reader will have to decide what is typical by reading as many oral histories as possible.

Why did they tell or remember what they did? It is clear that some of these memories represent strong emotional experiences. Fear explains a lot of the memories: fear of pounding seas, fear of close calls with freighters, fear of animals. But the uniqueness of the experiences, a uniqueness that became more apparent with the passage of time, also explains a lot of these stories. The nostalgia, evident in some sections, reveals that the experiences were unique and very pleasantly so.

The Times

Lighthouse keepers were given the responsibility of creating safety at sea. This was done by providing crucial location information to the mariner in a timely manner. By maintaining a beacon light, a fog horn, and later a radiobeacon, the keepers increased the information and improved the safety. But the tasks, responsibilities, technologies and lifestyles changed. The process in the 1930s was totally different from the process in the 1970s. Read Bill Simon's chapter to see just how much things had changed.

The major driving force of change was the conversion of energy source from kerosene and acetylene to electricity and solar. This evolution had a big impact on the skills and duties of the keepers. The time consuming task of caring for kerosene lamps was replaced by the equally time consuming attention required by the generators, compressors, and radiobeacons. But the use of electricity opened the safety at sea function to technological improvement. The steps in the process of creating safety were divided, refined, and in some cases, automated. By subdividing the tasks, some of the responsibility could be shifted from the lighthouse keepers to the mariners. By the 1950s the safety responsibility was jointly shared by the keeper and the boat captain who, as a team, made the system work. With further technological improvements the captain continued to take more responsibility and today the keeper is no longer a man but machines. Safety decisions are made onboard ship making the lighthouse keeper obsolete.

The change in technologies produced a second major change during this period, the change in staffing. Originally, the job of lighthouse keeper was a life-long profession. The job carried life and death responsibilities and the keepers were proud of their traditions and safety records. But as technology improved, the Coast Guard began to use young and inexperienced men at the light stations. Pride was being replaced by cost-effectiveness. Young keepers came and went. The lighthouse was no longer "home" but a "duty station." Three-year tours replaced 20-year tenures. The inspections were less frequent and less demanding. Pride in service was vastly diminished. Jim Collins was distraught when he returned to his lighthouse just a few years after leaving and saw the dirty floors.

By the 1970s the lighthouse hardships were removed. For nearly 100 years the keepers at Huron Island suffered the cold dampness of the stone house on the hill. They hand carried every bit of water they needed up 170 feet of treacherous rock. But the new, young Coast Guard persons found it easier to build a new wooden home near the lake shore. It was warmer, closer to the main work at the fog signal building and near drinking water. Their memories won't be the same. They won't be as romantic. The struggle was replaced by efficiency. There will be no children molded by this lighthouse experience. By 1983 all of the keepers were gone.

What does all this mean?

Times were changing and the participants seemed to know it.
Every person we talked to was proud of being a part of the lighthouse service. It is the kind of feeling that you sense with athletes. They are proud of being part of a winning team. Yes, there was hardship, privation, isolation but these were sacrifices needed to make the whole system excel. These people are also happy about the current interest in their lives. Most admit that they were lucky to have been involved. I think they all feel they are better for the sacrifices they made. They felt ownership in the system. They made history!

Transferring employment from the U. S. Lighthouse Service to the Coast Guard in 1939 was a serious matter. The Coast Guard did not have the same high-quality reputation as the Lighthouse Service. This was a thought provoking decision for each person. Certainly part of the decision was based upon pay, vacation, and retirement factors. But part was based purely upon reputation. Even as they were living it, these families knew that an era was passing.

Family life during the lighthouse era mattered to each of these individuals. This was a family endeavor. Every member had to play his or her part. The family, not just the keeper, got promoted. Although these employees enjoyed being promoted from 2nd to 1st assistant and then to keeper, it was not a daily factor in their lives. Spending time with their families was.

Thus you might wonder what effect this life style had on these people. Most went on to live ordinary lives. The rigors do not seem to have planted the seeds of leadership. The children grew up to be stable family members in society. For the most part these were people content with their station in life.

But nature has not changed.
Safety at sea is still a major concern. The power of nature has not been diminished nor controlled. Mariners still need the best possible information to make safe decisions while on the water. But today's information comes from electrical-powered systems that are removed from the adverse environment. A howling storm can extinguish a kerosene light, can interfere with commercially-powered electricity, but is not likely to effect the stored solar power of a battery light or the transmissions of a satellite. The romantic keepers, even the technician keepers, are gone. Technology prevails.

So what is the romance about?
Even these modern day keepers carried a large responsibility on their shoulders. Individually and collectively they mattered. Together they made a winning team. As family units they lived simple, wholesome, hard-working lives where right and wrong were clearly defined. Their impact was easily measured and it contained none of the fast-paced ambiguity of modern life. Who wouldn't want to live such a life? Let them take you back with their stories.

1

Stewart S. Edward

Civilian working out of Soo lighthouse depot
1936 to 1973
Interviewed December 12, 2003 by Sandy Planisek and Dick Moehl

Between 1936 and 1973 lighthouse technology underwent stupendous changes driven by the shift to electricity as a power source. During this time Stewart Edward evolved from a Lighthouse Service handyman into a Coast Guard civilian electrician. He was in the fortunate position to see and to participate in replacing the old acetylene systems with electrical systems.

Stewart was one of the corps of civilian experts that supplemented the skills of lighthouse keepers. These civilians worked for the Federal government but were not "coasties." Civilian positions still exist in the Coast Guard today.

Although cleaning, painting, and testing were part of his routine duties, Stewart mostly recalls the non-routine opportunities presented by moving from one light station to the next, dealing with changing electrical problems, and learning from the people and situations he encountered.

Thus Stewart is not a semi-reclusive light keeper. He is interested in change, he is interested in technology, he is focused on learning. In this interview he often criticizes his own behaviors in order to relay to me and to you the lessons he learned, the enduring lessons that carried him through his life's work of implementing change.

Stewart probably worked on as many different light stations as anyone. Therefore we must remember that one light station might blur with another, he saw a lot of them. But his recollections of the equipment are extremely clear. He certainly could rebuild the flasher mechanism today, at 94 years old. He still can debate the virtues of a 4-bulb changer vs. a 12-bulb changer. He knows the equipment.

I gained several new insights into the 20th century lighthouse world by talking to Stewart.

· First, it is impossible to generalize about anything during this period. Technology, regulations, and staff were constantly changing. The pace of change varied from location to location so that the circumstances at one station might be totally different at another.

· Second, lighthouses were no longer tended by romantic, kerosene-toting keepers checking their wicks. Keepers were moving from standing watch in the lantern to standing watch alongside a generator. The romance was disappearing.

· Third, there was room in the lighthouse service for all personality types. The secluded, introverted, generalist keeper now required support from the well-traveled, technically-skilled expert. And administration jobs grew exponentially under the new Coast Guard management.

While Stewart loved the isolation, solitude, and grand nature of lighthouses, he was basically interested in the challenges of change. He loved his job and still closely follows the technological changes of today's lighthouse world.

How did you get into the lighthouse service?
I took every civil service examination that came up that I figured I could pass. I passed quite a few. I had a lot of chances. I accepted the lighthouse service in 1936 because I didn't want to leave home. I was living in Dafter, Michigan.

I was born in Grosse Ile, Michigan in 1909. My middle name is St. Clair after the river. We left Detroit and ended up in Canada. I took all of my schooling in Canada. In 1925 my mother died and we moved from Canada to Dafter, Michigan. I was 16 years old and was grown up. Dad bought a little country store. That was where I got my start. That was where I was working when I filled out this examination and got called in. They would take the top three on the list. The first guy would not take the job because it was night work. The other guy would not take it because you got laid off in the fall. I was the third one and I took it.

Richard L. Moehl

What was the job?
Handyman. You were a helper and they classified you as a watchman. There were two of us. We worked in Sault Ste. Marie where the lighthouse depot was. That was the warehouse for the 11th lighthouse district. Our headquarters was in Detroit. Milwaukee was the 12th district, I think. There were the two of us at the Soo. At the office they had a manager and an office helper. Mac and I just worked in the yard raking or whatever needed done. I would work days and he would work nights. Hector McLean. He is gone. We

Stewart Edward outside his home with his lighthouse flag flying. He was given a lighthouse flag at retirement.

would change once a week. The guy that was on days would take a double shift so that the night guy could have a day off. The first years we were there we got laid off from the 15th of November until the 15th of April. This was without pay. The depot was open but our jobs weren't. The lakes were frozen over. We didn't get any road work that three years up till the Coast Guard took over in '39.

What light stations did you work at?
I worked at just about every lighthouse on Lake Superior. I didn't get to too many in the Apostle Island group. I did get to Rock of Ages, Stannard Rock, Huron Island. Then I came down to Escanaba, on the shore of Lake Michigan on that side. On this side of Lake Michigan I went down as far as Traverse City. On Lake Huron I came down as far as Port Huron. I was strictly maintenance.

Were you on a boat traveling all of the time?
No, no, no. Like going to Rock of Ages or Stannard Rock or those places, the keeper in Marquette would run me out on his little boat. I'd stay on the light until I got finished. If the light was on the mainland, I would take a truck and go.

On day shift we made up *Notice to Mariners* when we came in to work at 4 p.m. (notices of changes in navigational aids). We put them in envelopes and delivered

them to the post office at the locks for ships passing through and to Pittsburgh Supply Co. Then we took a 26-foot launch with an inboard engine and crossed the St. Marys River to the Canadian Ship Canal for ships going there. Well, McLean made one trip to show me where to go in Canada. He took me twice because I had never been in a boat or operated one before.

The first trip alone was almost my last. I got the engine going and got across

The white area is the territory covered by Stewart Edward out of the Sault Ste. Marie base

the river to the Canadian locks O.K. I started back. When I cleared the Canadian lock I noticed a large freighter coming upbound for the American locks. And to make matters worse, one was coming out of the American lock downbound. I envisioned myself caught between the two big freighters and momentarily panicked. I stalled my motor and started drifting down river. The battery was dead and I couldn't find the crank. I tried to get the oars loose and dropped one of the oar fittings. I finally located the crank and swung back towards the lock. By now my head had cleared up and I felt in control. But I was wondering what the wheelsman on the large freighter thought when he saw me. Good thing he didn't blow the horn at me as I might have rammed him. 😊

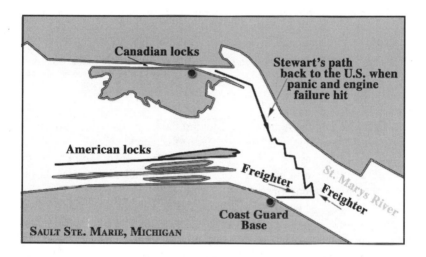

After the Coast Guard took over the service they wouldn't let me take the launch. They had their small packet boats and crew. They took me over once but they went through Canadian customs. The Canadians wouldn't let me take the boat up to the Canadian locks. They said, "Send the *Notice* by mail." That was the one and last time I delivered AtoN Notices (Aids to Navigation).

Things changed from the lighthouse service?
The old guy taught us when we first went in the lighthouse service. He said, "When you are in the office what you hear here stays here."

Stewart's Lessons
What you hear in the office stays in the office.

When you go out on a job you better make sure the light is lit when you leave. If you are working it in the daytime make sure it is operational for the night.

Stewart's Lessons
    When you leave the light make sure it is working properly.

Those are two things I always remembered.

What did they do at the depot?
In the daytime we would paint things, paint lights, work on lights. We had a big warehouse there. We were like a supply point for the upper lakes. We would be in there working on lights or on the buoys and stuff that was brought in for repair. That flasher there (pointing to a flasher sitting on his shelf) came out of White Shoals.

What's a flasher?
That's what operated the lights when I joined the Coast Guard. All of our lights on the river were acetylene. They operated off of acetylene gas. Our fog horns operated off of CO_2 gas. But this type of flasher gave them their characteristic. This could be adjusted to burn fixed or it could be burned up to 60 flashes per minute, or short then long flashes.

How does it work?
You hook up a tank of acetylene to your bottom changer. This sat inside the lens. You adjusted for your characteristic. See the two knobs? One is for length of time and the other is for length of flash or burning. You put 24 pounds of gas into it. You adjust that for the gas going to the top changer, set at 7.5 pounds of gas. When it hits 7.5 it trips, sending a shot of gas from the bottom changer up to the light. It had a little pilot on it all of the time. At that pressure it would send a shot of gas to the pilot. The light and dark period could be adjusted from regular flash to quick flash.

That flasher had two leather gaskets, one between each section. The leather gaskets, so some old-timers told me, were made from dog hides because dogs don't sweat.

The acetylene light was a beautiful light. The flame was pure white. It was in the shape of a fish tail. Some had three heads on them and some had more. The only ones I worked on had a single burn.

I spent some time with a flasher mechanic from the Buffalo district one season. Johnny O'Keef. He told me that over the years he had produced a similar flasher that operated off of acetylene gas. It could be made for less money than they were paying to AGA Co. But the higher ups turned his offer down. We had two types of flashers, one from AGA, but I can't think of the name of the other one. Of the two, I liked working on the AGA better.

Buoy lights came in every fall. They came off the buoy and into the shop. We would put them on the shelf bench and we would hook them up and check their characteristic and see if the pressure was right on both sides and replace the diaphragms in them when needed. Then they were put back on next spring. That gradually changed.

White Shoal's flasher with a single head

Things changed around when the Coast Guard took over. Our schedule and work changed. Mac and I got work every day on a 40-hour week. We had a shop for all of our repairs to come in. We took care of the lights. When the buoys came in he took the lights off. We would paint the lights up again and get them all ready to go back.

How did you learn to do this?
We had a book. It would tell you what to do and how to do it.

Did you join the Coast Guard when it took over?
No, they gave us that choice but they didn't have much use for Mac or me because neither one of us had a profession. We weren't a machinist, we weren't a full-fledge electrician. Whoever retired, if it was an electrician, they would get one off the market. That way we stayed where we were. We turned out pretty good. We got a lot of travel and we always got paid for traveling.

You couldn't stay in the lighthouse service?
The best offer was as a seaman. No, we were both married and had a family, at a seaman's pay . . . They gave us a choice to stay on as a civilian. We stayed as civilians. We did all right.

What was the salary in 1936?
I made $110 a month. It was pretty good.

When the Coast Guard took over from the Lighthouse Service, after a while, changes were made. McLean and I had been operating a 100-watt radio. The fellow on day shift broadcast AtoN information from 10 a.m. to 10:15 a.m. and the fellow on nights broadcast from 10 p.m. to 10:15 p.m. Any of our men out on the lights in need of material could call in to Soo Base and have us pick it up and

Stewart Edward at age 94

Richard L. Moehl

a tender would deliver it. Well, one night Bruce Miller called in from Stannard Rock with a list and there was quite a bit of static. I can't recall what the item was but Bruce couldn't make out what I was saying, so I had heard others on the air, when static was bad, say *B* before Box Set. Well I had to try and get Bruce to make out what the word was so I started out, *"P as in P in Pot."* Well the next night when I came to work the first thing I heard was P as in P in Pot. I think every station on the air heard that.

A friend who had a set told Mac and me that by shifting our dial a couple of points we could talk to other stations, especially at night. Well, we did and were talking to other stations until about a month later Mac and I were called into the office and a stranger was there from the head office. He was from Washington and wanted to see our license to operate a radio station. We didn't have one. He then went on to explain what the penalty was for operating an unlicensed station. But seeing as how it was a Coast Guard communication system with their ships and stations, we could convey weather and aids to navigation emergencies, but no more shift chats.

The Coast Guard moved their office and radio equipment to the lighthouse office and warehouse. They took over our system. Our hours were changed to daytime, 8-hour days unless we were on the road. The Lighthouse Service had four main field men. McLean and I were mainly on base repairing buoys and equipment. When one of our main field men went on a job and required a helper they would send Mac or me with them. Eventually we would be in a position to take over their place when they retired. I had the chance to work at one time or another with Bruce Miller, Dave Wilson, and Jones. Dave was the official hard hat diver in the Lighthouse Service. McLean was his helper and when Dave retired Mac took over.

I had the battery and electrical shop for repairing flashers, etc. and also testing new AtoN equipment. My shop was in the basement of one of the barracks. When new items came in I would set them up in the shop and test them. When I retired we were running tests on a fog detector system. This could be adjusted to turn on a fog signal when visibility was 3 miles, more or less. It sent a beam that triggered the fog signal when fog or snow moved in.

When did you get out of the service?
The third day of February of 1973.

Radiobeacon clock

Tell us about the clock.
Radiobeacons operated off of the gauge down the side. There were three stations involved. One station would come on here at, say, midnight for a minute. Then it would shift to another lighthouse and the next lighthouse would come back on. It would give you triangulation on your passenger ships when you were going up and down the river.

This is the clock that they set the radiobeacon to?
These clocks would turn the radio on. Can you see these marks – 1, 2, 3? You have three lighthouses. This one comes

Stewart and his Seth Thomas clock that ran the radiobeacon

on for a minute and then goes off the air. Then lighthouse two would come on and then go off the air. Then three would come on and go off the air. Then the fourth time it would go back and start over. That way the ships coming up would receive the different readings so they could locate their position.

Did this go on continuously or just at the beginning of the hour?
The clock ran all of the time.

It didn't trigger the radiobeacon all of the time?
No, no. Just when required. When I first started in 1936 every night at midnight they would set the clocks with the Washington time signal.

What is this on the side?
These are your relays. They are connected to your beacon equipment. When the clock comes on it reaches down here and turns the switch on. That activates the beacons. But the beacon won't come on until it is scheduled for up here. It will come on for every third minute.

What is powering this clock?
It was hand wound.

This came out of Rock of Ages?
Rock of Ages, yeah. When they automated stuff they got rid of these old hand wound clocks and put in electric clocks. So you don't have to wind them.

What does this knob do?
That has something to do with adjusting your time, if the clock was running slow or running fast. This clock just quit running about 2 or 3 months ago. This cable finally started wearing out. So I attempted to put a new one in. I bought eight feet of this kind of cable and put it on. I hadn't stopped to think that it has to be put on one way. I didn't get it on the right way. To make a long story short I made a mistake somewhere.

Huron Island

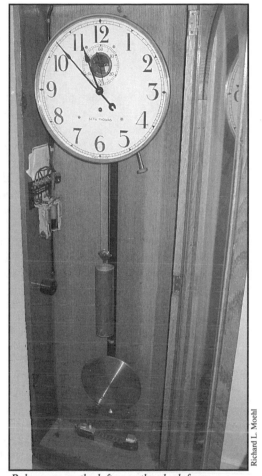

Richard L. Moehl

Relays are on the left near the clock face

Did you live in the Sault at the base?
No, I lived out at Dafter. The lighthouse had so many civilians. They had a civilian mechanic, electrician, carpenter. Occasionally a job would come up that they needed a hand. They would take either Mac or me with them. That's when we started to learn. The first job I went on Frank Beisel took me out to Huron Island.

The fog signal building is on one end of the island and the light is on the other end. We had some work to do out there. I think we were changing the air compressors. The tender unloaded the material on the dock. They brought the equipment up from the dock to the fog signal building on the railroad track. When they took them off on the top they sat them on the left hand side of the track. So Beisel and I went up to put them in. We had to jack them up again and lay them on the right side of the track to get them in.

You always learn from the other guy. We jacked the old ones up a little bit and sat them on some blocks. Beisel said to go out and get a 4-inch block. I went out and cut two 2 by 4s for the block. I cut two little pieces. (Laugh) I can still hear him. I took them back in and gave them to him. He threw them across the room, "I want a 4-inch block!" I went back out and got a 4-inch block. He was mad. He said I want to tell you, if I put those two blocks there and you start jacking this thing up one of them is going to slip and someone is going to get hurt. If I put the 4-inch block there it will not slip. That's how you learn.

What was his name again?
Frank Beisel. He died too. He was the head man. I was just the helper. Then we had to run new cables from the fog signal building up to the lighthouse. They sent two of us up there to do that. It must be 3/4 of a mile or more to haul that cable.

Do you know what year this was?
Oh, Lord no. That is something I have regretted ever since. We always had travel orders. You always had work orders. When we left up home I got rid of them all.

Huron Island fog signal at left and lighthouse at top right of picture

Who was the lighthouse keeper at Huron Island then?
I don't remember. He lived in that little village there.

Was the village Skanee?
Yes, but I can't remember his name. He fed us when we were on the lights like that. He was the cook.

We talked about Dick Campbell's memories of Huron Island and Steward continued.
When you come in where the boat house was, down below, it was 100 or 110 steps up. When Rogers and I were out there we would sit on the back porch there and feed the rabbits. You'd sit there and after a while they would finally come up and eat out of your hand. A wildcat got on that island one year, one winter and didn't get off. It cleaned the rabbits out. That was quite an island. I'd like to go to the garbage dumps on those islands. The things you would find. They got the idea one time to put AC generators out there. They put three. I could never figure how they figured three were going to work. They are fortunately set up in such a way that as one failed the next one would kick in, and the next one kick in, until you got the first one fixed. I don't know how that worked out, whether it worked or not. That was when they were trying to make it unwatched. They would be hooked up to big fuel tanks.

The signature step is dated 1951 and it lists E. Kohns, C. Kane, H. McLean, F. Stephans, W. Seppala, S. Edward. It sits on a stone marked Mesquite '48.

I'm sending a couple of snap shots for your album. The one with the names in concrete was taken on Huron Island when a crew from the Soo Base was working on the boat house and the boat tracks below the lighthouse. Six of us were out there and we had to do our own cooking. One meal the guy had oyster stew. I didn't like oysters so one of the keepers said, "I've got a pot of stew cooking, help yourself." Well I dipped into the pot and came up with a fish head – eye to eye. That was one meal I skipped.

Rock of Ages

Would it take several days?
I spent almost six weeks on Rock of Ages one fall. That was a heck of a place to be. A storm come up.

What were you there to do?
We were doing everything. All odd jobs. But the weather just didn't work for us. It was late in the fall, that was the bad part of it.

You are shaking your head, what was so bad about it?
I remember when we ran out of food. We had hot dogs and Bisquick. Food ran awful low.

When you went out to a light station did you bring enough food for yourself?
The station that took us out, what was it, Portage Station, the station right there at the head of the Keweenaw waterway.   Yeah, Portage Station would take us out there.

Boat ride to Rock of Ages

Would you take your own food?

No, when they knew we were coming out they always took enough. We only took food to unmanned stations.

How many went with you then?

Two of us went over, plus the crew that was at the light. We worked on the generators. We worked on the air compressors. Just everything.

When we were sent out to the lights for repair work or new installations, we generally got bunks up in the tower near the top where the fog horns were located. The second night at Rock of Ages, fog set in around 2 a.m. and the keeper started the fog horns. When the fog horn blasted off I almost hit the ceiling. The fog lasted 36 hours. It got so, as time

Richard L. Moehl

Laundry hanging to dry at Rock of Ages

went by, the horns could blow and you would sleep right through but the minute they quit you would wake. The same thing would happen if the generator or the air compressors stopped. You could sleep right through them running, but when they quit you would wake up.

When you went to a station was it typical that you had a kit and just repaired all of the equipment? A general tune-up?

Most of the time when we went to the lights it was for a purpose. Something was wrong. That is why we would travel with one of these foreman and we would pick it up (learn from him). Because in the lighthouse service if someone at the top retired, if you qualified, you would gradually move up. That all changed when the Coast Guard took over. There was a different system.

What other lighthouses did you go to on Lake Superior?
I went all the way up to Grand Marais, Minnesota. Duluth.

Who had you come out and repair a lens?
We didn't repair lenses. No. We just did equipment. That lens at White Shoals is a beautiful lens. Three million candle bar. The best light on the lakes.

I thought the crew at the station repaired their own generators.
A lot of times they weren't qualified so we would go out and work on them. One of the lights on Lake Michigan, I forget which, had DC generators. The old generators were all DC, greasy and all that stuff. This one was not quite working right. They sent me out there to redo the wiring in it. I disconnected the wires and I put markers on them. I disconnected over at the panel. I put my new wires in, (laugh), brought them all back to the generator and hooked them up. I threw the switch and BANG. It kicked out. Then I was lost. So I took the panel covers off again. I tried to figure out what the hell I did wrong. The chief came down. He said, "You got a problem?" I think I have. He said, "Come up and have a cup of coffee." OK. "You get a cup of coffee and maybe it will clear it up." So I went up and had a cup of coffee with him. We sat there and talked for a few minutes. I went back down and it did clear up. I'd made a change in one little wire. I marked it for four and I thought it was a four. I'd got some grease on it and I got it mixed up with a seven. If I hadn't of greased it over I would have been all right. I changed it and I was all set. That was kind of nice, instead of bawling you out, say have a cup of coffee. Somehow it felt pretty good.

You get out on some of the lights and the fishermen would go by. You give them a 5-gallon bucket of fuel oil and they would give you a bucket of whitefish. We used to have a lot of whitefish dinners on the stations.

Did you go by boat to some of these offshore lights?
If it was an offshore light the Coast Guard would take me out.

You didn't have your own boat at the depot?
No, we had trucks for transportation. Like if we were going to Beaver Island, we would take the ferry to Beaver Island. But we could take our truck over.

Let's talk about the changes that happened to the equipment at the lighthouses.

When I started, all the lights in the St. Marys River were acetylene. Some of the range lights were acetylene. Some of the range lights were the old locomotive head light style with a round face and a reflector back. We changed them to railway signals, with a double light. The first change from acetylene was to wet cells, batteries, DHB batteries. You had to put in acid and water. The next change was to air cells.

Lake trout dinner at Rock of Ages

Richard L. Moehl

How did you charge up the batteries?
We brought them in. If they were set well enough they would run the season. They would come back every fall.

When the batteries would come in, in the fall, they would come in to the shop. As many as 1,000 would be taken out of the racks and recharged. We had a great big tank that would hold 16 batteries. We would put them in this tank and fill it with water and wash them to get the acid off. Then we would take them out and scrape them and paint them. Then we would re-rack them for next spring.

Stewart sent several letters after the initial interview. This one says,

"the Windmill project was a test, not on buoys, but on fixed structures like range lights. McLean had that project. They were trying to find a new type operation from acetylene to electric - using batteries for power + tried the windmills to see if they could keep the batteries charged up.
It didn't work out."

You were painting the batteries?
Yes, they were metal cells. The battery was in a metal case and this plastic case sat down inside. We had to keep a record on each battery. We had about 1,000 batteries.

The next type of battery we went to was air cells for post lights and solid lights on the river, on a solid position on piers and stuff like that, not on a buoy. They were a one-time battery. We would take them out and if you had it figured out right they would run you the season. You just threw them away.

St. Marys River

The man who lived in a white house next to where the Sugar Island Ferry docked was a Mr. Mihlethaler, at Little Rapids Cut. He had a boat and he had a little house. The house was only about 700 feet from a city water line but the city wouldn't put the line in unless the Lighthouse Service paid for it. So when the attendant lived there they had a small electric pump and pumped river water for the house use and carried water from the city system for drinking purposes. The Coast Guard, when they took over, sent McLean and me down there to put in a well. We jetted a pipe down about 110 feet and got water but it was salty. Later on they did connect to the city system.

Back to Mihlethaler. He had a stretch of the St. Marys River to watch. Any ship that would report a light out would call us at the base. We would call Mihlethaler and he would get his boat and take us. Regardless of night or day he would go. There was a light attendant at Middle Neebish. There was an attendant at Little Rapids Cut. Each attendant had a boat. For any outages we would just call them and they would go and do it.

The Lighthouse Service had a system like a report card and once a year you would be graded on how well you performed your duties. Mihlethaler always had a Very Good report on his card. He was close to retirement and would get $150.00 a month. Well his last report was signed by the C.O. Coast Guard when they took over from the Lighthouse Service. He signed Mihlethaler's card as Good. When that went in, the Lighthouse Service Department reduced his pension to $125.00. The Coast Guard felt real bad and tried everything to get it changed but couldn't. When Mihlethaler retired his assistant, R. Haynes, lived at Barbeau Pt. A Mr. Hugh Cook took over Mihlethaler's spot.

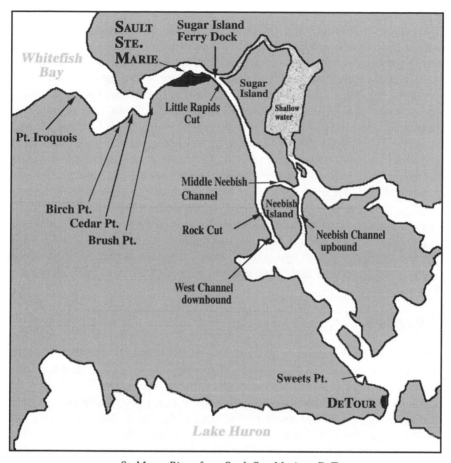

St. Marys River from Sault Ste. Marie to DeTour

How far down the river did you go?
DeTour. We went down the West Channel and back up the Neebish Channel to catch the buoys on both sides. There was a keeper on Neebish Island, a light attendant, one at Little Rapids Cut, one at West Neebish. Three light attendants. The Little Rapids Cut one would take care of lights above the locks at the Sault. We had the Vidal Shoals Lights which we took care of from the Soo. They are on the Soo locks grounds. Others were Brush Point, Cedar Point, and Birch Point above the locks. Each had a family dwelling. Later on, when commercial power became available, they were converted to that source of power and were handled by maintenance men (McLean and me) until the Coast Guard took over.

Did you ever hear about "dead air" from anyone sailing the Great Lakes? On the St. Marys River, between DeTour and Pt. Iroquois there were (I don't know about now) 8 fog bells – 6 rang by hand from a lookout Coast Guard tower. A line was attached to the bell clapper and, with the use of a stop watch, the guy in the tower would ring the bell once every 15 or 30 seconds in fog or heavy snow fall when visibility was poor. There were two bell floating buoys with bells activated by wave action. One, on a crib light above DeTour, operated off CO_2 gas. It was located on Sweets Point Crib. This one operated continuously and was unmanned. One time in the early '40s I was sent down to Sweets Pt. to check the system that had failed. It had been decided to remove the CO_2 system and provide a battery operated striker. We made the change over in a couple of days and left the bell ringing. When we were some distance from the bell we stopped to make sure it was operating and couldn't hear anything. Back we went to correct it, but before we got there we could hear it. But just to be sure everything was OK we double checked and it was operating correctly. That's when the old-timer we had hired to get us out there with the equipment told us there were dead spots in the air. Hard to believe.

West Neebish

West Neebish had a rear range light like the one in Cheboygan. The West Neebish had a rear tank house that they used for their acetylene tanks and paint and stuff like that. They sent two of us to put this new range light up. We had to carry all our tools and material about half mile from the road, and it took us all day to pack stuff in so the next day we would have a full day to change things over. We left our lunches in the little shack. We were working doing this and doing that. We heard a little noise once and a while but I thought it was something that dropped. Come around lunch time I said to the guy, "Do you want to go down and get our lunch?" He said, "No." So I went down. I didn't get down. Before I got there a doggone bear came up. He didn't get our lunch. We must have rattled something and scared him. He had walked through some mud and his hind feet seemed that long (about 8 inches). They probably weren't. No I didn't see him. But we heard that noise. I often wondered if the other guy didn't see him and that was the reason he didn't want to go down.

When I retired I went back to the St. Marys River one day. The fellow asked, "Would you like to go check the lights?" I said, "Yeah." I took a ride. I was surprised, where we used to have big racks of batteries, they have a little solar panel there now.

The Coast Guard had a lookout at West Neebish Channel. They had one, two, three, four, five lookouts on the river there, that boats would report. The one at the head of the Rock Cut shot a beam straight up. It must have been some kind of fog light or something. I never saw it in operation.

Cheboygan

Did you ever get to Cheboygan?
I worked out of Cheboygan quite a few times. I worked on the range lights there at Cheboygan.

Did it start as acetylene?
Not when I worked on it. There was shore (power) right there. They wanted to replace the front one and the back one. They sent a young seaman with me. He wouldn't climb the back one.

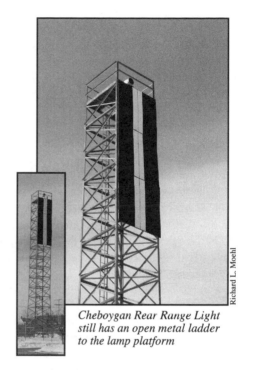

Richard L. Moehl

Cheboygan Rear Range Light still has an open metal ladder to the lamp platform

I can understand that, the rear tower is a little scary.
What do you mean scary? The ladder was on the outside. There was no safety outfit. The *Mackinaw* was there then. We could never get the new lights lined up. When we checked them we could never get the doggone things lined up. So we set everything right back the way it was. Whatever was wrong with them, they would not line up like the skipper wanted them. We took them down and put the old ones back.

The skipper of the Mackinaw *was the one complaining about them?*
I don't know who was complaining but he was the one who checked them for us.

What kind of lights were there and what kind were you trying to put in?
It was practically the same light, it was an electric light, but it wasn't so big or clumsy.

Stannard Rock

What places got generators and what places got batteries?
We had AC (alternating current) generators at Alpena, at Thunder Bay Island. I think they were the only AC generators I can remember. Stannard Rock had a battery bank.

Why different ones there?
I have a better memory on the DC (direct current) ones. The DC generators were the original ones. You had DC generators and DC air compressors. That was original equipment. We had a bank of 54 batteries. Yes 54, 2-volt cells. You had the same thing at Rock of Ages. Glass cells. At Stannard Rock we put in a new bank. Those glass batteries weighed 50 or 60 pounds each. At Stannard Rock and Spectacle Reef, the lights are both the same, they were built the same year – 1872, the stairway is in the wall. You walk up and you walk across the room and you go half a circle up. So they sent me up to Stannard Rock to put in a new battery bank. I got out there. Here the batteries were all down on the cement. How in the heck am I going to get them up. You can't carry them, 54 cells.

I'll have to have some help to get the 54 batteries to the top. He gave me a man to help me. We made a cradle for one battery. You have to watch as you go up the stairway. One guy has to back up. So I went up there and I disconnected one cell. I realized that I'd never have this done by night. We carried one down. The chief said something, "You know the last time the batteries were changed we used that skiff out there. We put two or three batteries in it. You see that hook up there? We hook that up and we start our engine here. We pull the skiff up with two or three and we take them in the window and then we take three or four down." I said, "Why in the HMMM didn't you tell me.?" He said, "You know I've learned one thing since I've been out here. You fellows you come out here and you think you know it all. So one way to let you find out is to let you try." That's another thing I never forgot.

Do you remember the name of the tender that took you out?
It wasn't a lighthouse tender that took me out. It was one of the Coast Guard ships. The old *Amaranth* was out of Duluth. The *Aspen* was out of Sault Ste. Marie. The *Marigold* was out of Detroit. The *Hollyhock* was out of Milwaukee. The *Amaranth* would come out to the Soo and get their supplies and take them out to the

---

Stewart's Lessons
Never be too proud to ask for help.

---

various lights on Lake Superior on the way back (to Duluth). The *Aspen* was replaced by the *Tamarack*. The *Aspen* was an old steam job, steam engine. The *Tamarack* was diesel.

St. Helena

Do you remember St. Helena? It had an acetylene light. Was it there when you started there?

No, we were the ones who went down there and changed it. Me and Hubert Rogers, in the Sault. They sent Hubert and me out there to remove all acetylene gear from the light tower and replace the light with a battery-operated electric flasher with a 4-bulb lamp changer. We went out and we took batteries. No persons were living on the island so we decided to take blankets, food and a plumber's furnace to cook with and stay right on the island. The Coast Guard dropped us off at the old boat house and said they could pick us up on Friday in time to get home for the weekend. We were both used to being dropped off. I don't know how long the lighthouse had been empty.

We got up there. We thought, where would we sleep? We finally settled on going down in the basement. The doors and the windows upstairs were all gone. We got a bunch of cedar boughs and we made ourselves mattresses. We cooked our supper on the plumber's furnace using a sheet of metal we found for a stove top. We had bacon, eggs, fried potatoes, coffee and donuts. We checked out the basement door and found the hinges were broken so the only thing we could do was stand it in place and lean a post against it to hold it. So we had supper. That was the only time I carried a gun. I took a .38 caliber pistol with me. I don't know why, but I did. Having fried bacon I was scared about bears prowling around and the smell of bacon bringing them in. Well, I took the pistol out of the box and put it under my pillow. Hubert got in the back bed, with me in the front. During the night the wind got up and it blew the door down. When the door came down it made a heck of a racket. I started rummaging around under the pillow for my pistol. My buddy said, "What the heck are you trying to do? You are likely to shoot me!" My first thought was of a bear. It wasn't a bear and I didn't shoot anybody. The next night we made sure the door was secure and I left the gun out in the tool box. We took the acetylene equipment out and put a battery operation in there. Air cell batteries.

St. Helena overgrown in 1987

Do you remember when this was?
No. It was after the Coast Guard took over. It was vacant a long time because everything was gone. The windows and doors. That was too bad. The best of material in them. That's a beautiful building. Go down in the basement and see our boughs. The roof was pretty good when we were there. That is why we looked upstairs. There was a farmer on there at one time. There were apple trees.

Acetylene

How big were the acetylene tanks?
Regular. Just like for welding. It was part of Mac's and my job, every year a tender would bring up a load of new tanks from Detroit before we started getting them from the Sault. We had rails set up. We had a hot water tank that we cut in two for a trough. When these tanks all came in they had to be checked for leaks. We would roll a tank in. We had lines underneath it. There are two or three blind plugs on them. There is one right up on the shoulder and there is one on the base. All of our tools were brass so there were no sparks. We had a real fine punch. The blind plugs were the size of a match. You put the tanks in the trough and see

them leaking. You'd tap and seal them. We would run through 200 tanks like that and put them back on the rack. As each tender came in and wanted new ones they would take a load of ours and leave the old ones for us to fix.

How long would a tank last?
I couldn't tell you. Some buoys had two tanks. Some had three tanks.

Were you changing the tanks constantly during the season?
They were supposed to last all season. Everything was set up based on the size of the light and the characteristic, the number of tanks that was going to be in it. Most of the buoys took two or three tanks.

Did you ever work on the sun relay?
The sun relay was a round glass tube. It is a solid black shaft with a glass cover. In the daylight, when the sunlight comes out, that black draws the heat. It expands, pushes down, and shuts it off. At night when it gets dark, it shrinks. When it shrinks, it turns back on. They had them on range lights. They had them on some buoys. This type worked with either gas or electric.

What were the problems with the switches? Were they hard to keep going? Why did they switch to batteries?
It was more convenient, instead of hauling them big acetylene tanks. At Neebish, on the range lights, they had to haul those things half mile or more. The batteries held up pretty good. I never saw many batteries on our range lights though. Most of them were operated off of acetylene. Some of them were close enough to have commercial power. But that relay would work good on them. The last one I knew was over in Copper country, a little town. With the battery-operated lights they sent in new light relays. They are about the size, a little bigger than your thumb. They were installed right in the light. They were tied into your light circuit and would turn the light on and off.

The first battery ones were also sunlight activated?
Oh yeah. They were put in up at Ontonagon. It had a red lens. The relay wouldn't work inside the red lens. Automation is a funny thing. It doesn't always work.

GLLKA is going to be taking care of the light in St. James Harbor.
My buddy and I went out there one time years ago. Something was wrong with the light (Beaver Head). The boat was late getting there. We didn't get out there until just about dark. We drove up to the house. There was a car parked out there. This was in the fall. Nobody said anyone was here. So we walked in and here are

four guys sitting at the table having supper, cooking steaks. I said we are going to go up and check the light and fix it. I looked down and I said, "I've seen you on TV." He said, "No that is my brother." He was a weather announcer or something on TV. I know darn well it was him. They had a grant or an option or something from the Coast Guard that they could use the lighthouse as a camp for the fall, for hunters. He invited us, we got a steak supper out of it.

Did you ever do anything on the light right there by the boat? (St. James)
The only thing we did there was change the light or flasher in the tower. That's a nice little island. At night, when most lights would turn on at one time, the lights would dim. Not enough power!

What was the worst thing to happen to you during your lighthouse service years?
I had a lot of good times. I used to like going on the lighthouses. I did. Offshore lights. Some of the young guys would come out there and they were lost. They couldn't see it, 18 or 19 year old guys, used to city life. Like Stannard Rock. I used to like going to Stannard Rock at night in the fall. Sit up there in the light, the number of birds that came around, out of this world. I saw birds up there that I never saw on shore. I liked that work.

Also lots of rough weather. I only got seasick once, in a small boat. It wasn't too bad on the big boats. I liked the small boats.

Lansing Shoals

We went to Lansing Shoals. We left Lansing Shoals and we were supposed to go back to Charlevoix at 7 o'clock. We got as far as Beaver Island and a storm came up, fog and wind and everything. It got foggy. We got off track some way or another. I said to the

Northern Lake Michigan

guy, "The compass is off." "Well which way is it off?" I said, "We were going with the storm. Call Lansing Shoal and get a reading on it someway." He said, "There is a fog bell out here somewhere." So we found the fog bell. But you know when you get out there you hear the sound. You get over there, the doggone bell is over here. We wound up 10 o'clock that night at Petoskey. We saw the shore lights of Petoskey and that is where we landed.

Skillagalee

We went out there one night, another guy and myself. We were out to change the equipment in the lamp, in the tower. We took a fourth order lens out of there. We went to remove the lens and acetylene equipment and replace it with a 12-volt D.C. battery-operated light flasher and lamp changer assembly with an AGA daylight control. This turned the light on when it got dark and off at daybreak. The house was there then at Skillagalee. There was a pretty nice house there then. It was practically automated when we were there. There was nobody in the house. Since then they knocked it all down.

We had to go to the Charlevoix Coast Guard Station to have the station boat drop us off with our material while they were on their way to Beaver Island; they were supposed to pick us up the next day on their way back. The weather bureau man had some weather instruments on Skillee so he rode out with us. Somehow, the boat forgot to stop on the way back. Later on in the afternoon, a storm started up and a boat couldn't get in with the waves picking up. The house was dry but there was no heat so we chose an outside corner out of the wind, picked up a pile of driftwood, and started a fire to take the chill out of our bones. There was nothing left to eat.

At about 9:30 p.m. we heard a Coast Guard 40-footer coming toward the island. We finally made voice contact and it was the boat from the Beaver Island Station. He couldn't come in too close due to the low water around Skillee. We had a small flat-bottom boat which we used to bring in the materials from the larger boat. It was either use the boat or wade out. He had a good searchlight and could pick us up. We had to wade and push our flat-bottom boat until we were waist high before he could stop his boat long enough for us to climb over the side into his. It was a cold rough ride to Beaver Island and hard to find a place to stay and dry out. About one year later, the Coast Guard demolished the dwelling because young folks were making a party island out of Skillee.

Do you know where the lens went?
I haven't any idea. If there was some way to find where those old log books were.

A fourth order lens you can pick it up and take it out?
Yes, you can pick it up but not as easy as you think. They are heavy. We had the two types - the bulls-eye type and the bell type. In the bell type the light flashed. In the bulls-eye type the lens rotated.

Gull Rock Light

It was the only lighthouse I recall that I worked on that just had a light and no other Aids to Navigation equipment. This lighthouse showed a flashing red light, 170 candle power, every three seconds. The flash was 0.3 seconds long. I don't have any information regarding the date it was placed in an unmanned operation. My first trip to this light was to correct an outage report. The light source was provided from acetylene gas operating a K-130 AGA flasher mechanism. The lighthouse had been closed for some time and when we approached it in a 26-foot launch from Manitou Island station it looked like a house sitting on a gravel knoll, lots of small stones and gravel. I found a large agate, about the size of a lemon, behind the house. I had it sliced into several pieces later on. When we went into the kitchen section, one wall had all the names of the crew of the lighthouse tender *Amaranth*.

A few years later I removed the acetylene equipment and replaced the light equipment with battery-powered equipment.

The toilet was built of brick and located just at the water line. Every time a storm came up the waves washed the toilet clean. This was better than some isolated stations where I worked. Some had outside toilets and were built in such a way that once in a while they took a horse and pulled out a compartment, hauled it back in the timber, emptied it into a pit, cleaned it out and returned it to the structure. This job usually fell to the lowest man at the station.

This was the only off-shore light where a man and wife were keepers.

My last time to Gull Rock was on the tender *Sundew* when we changed the batteries and flasher mechanism. The skipper sent six of us into the light with the ship's work launch. The launch could only go in so close. Then we had a flat bottom boat the rest of the way. A storm blew in from the northwest and we had a rough time getting back to the work boat. It was the first time for me to be in a small

Michigan Lighthouse Conservancy

Gull Rock Lighthouse

boat that dropped into the trough and I could see water higher than my head in front and back of us. The captain swung the tender around in such a manner that we came in on the calm side. It was quite an experience – and a wet one!

Did you maintain clockworks, was that part of your job?
No. They put in different equipment. No. I don't know if any men were working on them. Things were changing.

Whitefish Point

The White Shoals lens is at Whitefish Point.
I was there (Whitefish Point). I could never see it. We put in two DC beacons, airplane beacons. They had them set at an angle in order to duplicate the characteristic. I installed a light relay so that if one bulb burned out the bulb would change in time enough that the characteristic would show up. After they put that up we got a heck of a northwest storm. In order to get the characteristic they had to set the lights at an angle. The northwest storm was so strong it would stall the light. They were adjustable for tightness. They called about 10 o'clock at night. We had to go up there to change the tension so it would operate with the proper flash.

We were at Sturgeon Point, they have a display of bulbs on a teeter totter changer. Did you ever put those in?

Yes, we got them. Two bulbs. Some were a round bulb and others were a tall slim bulb. We had a Wallace and Tiernan lamp changer at Crisp Point. It had 12 bulbs in it. It worked off of batteries. I didn't

Whitefish Point 1966

think they really showed up good. I had the skipper check it when we took the big lens out and put this different one in. He spotted it on his way up and he said it showed up good at night. That would use 12 bulbs but most of our lamp changers had the four bulbs.

Did you have to go out and check the lights from a boat?

Most of that stuff we checked in the shop, to get the alignment.

They say the lighthouse lenses shoot the beam out horizontally. But it can't be horizontal because nobody could see it. So it's slightly angled down, right?

You set the bulb in the lens. Next you sight through the center of your light source and through your lens. Then adjust your bulb up or down until your bulb filament and lens line up to the horizon. If your bulb is too high it sends the beam down or if too low sends the beam up. I hope this is clear.

MULTIPLE LAMPCHANGER
TYPE FU-847

Voltage: 6-16 D.C.
Capacity: 17 - S.C. Pref. Base
           S-11 or S-8 Lamps
           8 - S.C. Pref. Base
           G-16½ Lamps

HEAVY DUTY LAMPCHANGER ·   HEAVY DUTY LAMPCHANGER
        TYPE FA-80   TYPE FA-148

Capacity: 2 Mogul Bi-Post Base Lamps			
Arrangement	Voltage	Cycles	Wattage
FA-80011	32	60	1500
FA-80021	32	25	1500
FA-80031	115	60	1500
FA-80041	115	25	1500
FA-80131	115	60	1000

Voltage:	110 AC-DC
Wattage:	1000
Capacity:	4 Mogul Screw
	Base Lamps

Stewart Edward's Wallace and Tiernan manual

I remember the district office in Cleveland sending us a new type range light, one that wouldn't require two lights like we had. I set the system up in our shop and put in a 4-bulb lamp changer and turned it on. I got it set and adjusted but when I changed bulbs it threw it out of focus. I changed it back to the previous bulbs and it operated right. Well, I went to the office and told the C.O. the problem and he said sit down, I'll call the District. He did and explained what happened and they said, "Your man doesn't know what he is doing. Set up a meeting and I'll be up there and check it out." He arrived the next day and made arrangements with the base to have one of our tenders take him out to Whitefish Bay at night and he would check it out. He flew in. We (two of us) took a panel truck up to Cedar Point. I installed lights and batteries and took along a hand radio so we could communicate. The tender went up the bay. He called to turn the light on. We did. He crossed the range line and it was red on one side, red on the other side, and fixed white in the center. He said change lamps so we advanced the lamp changer to bring a new bulb into place. We did and he said, "You moved the light." We said we didn't because the light is bolted to a steel plate. He said turn it back. So we tripped the changer and brought the original bulb in focus and turned it on. This checked O.K. Now change bulbs. We did and all I could hear was, "- - - - take it back to the shop." I don't know where the light went and I never heard any more about it.

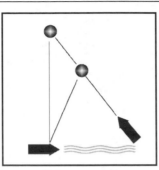

With the range light system a boat travels with an eye on both lights. When they line up over one another the boat then turns for the approach.

With the single, multi-colored light the boat would watch the red light zone gradually be replaced by the white light. When the light was completely white the boat would turn and approach.

White Shoals

That is another thing about White Shoals. They had a telephone line to Lansing Shoals. Lansing Shoals had a telephone line to the weather bureau in Sault Ste. Marie. White Shoals would call Lansing and give him the weather report that they have. Then Lansing would phone both reports into the weather bureau in the Sault. It also gave us guys out there on temporary duty a way to call home and let the folks know when we would be home. The weather had a lot to do with us getting off the light.

Was there a line that ran on the bottom of the lake?
Yeah, a telephone cable.

The Coast Guard had their own telephone system They always used to get new telephone poles. They came in at the Sault in a gondola. That's a coal car in the railroad. We would go up there and unload them. We had a little tow motor with a boom on it. They sent three of us, the chief to run the machine and two of us to handle the lines. We made a sling with one of us on each end of the car. We would put our chain around maybe four poles or five poles. Then the chief would swing them out. We would line the boom up so the poles would come down in a pile. This time I reached up and the next time I woke up in the hospital.

Another old-timer once told me, "Never trust a chain." If you are going to do something use a cable or a rope. Both of them will start to give and you can see it. When a chain breaks, it breaks. There is no stretch and then break. And that is what happened. The chain on my end broke. I often wonder. Sometimes you never listen to what you are told. They went down and picked me up and put me into the car, we had a little car. We got to the hospital and the hospital wouldn't take me in. The chief said, "He is hurt." They had to get the commander to come up before they would take me in. The only time I remember afterwards was when I was on the table in the room and the doctor was doing something to me. I said I wanted to go home. He said you can't go home. He pushed me down twice. I kept saying I want to go home. He said, "OK, go home." So I rolled half way over to go home. The next time I woke up I was in bed and I was tied up so tight I couldn't even breathe.

Stewart's Lessons
Never trust a chain.

The logs fell and hit you?
Yeah, it tore one of my ears half off. Broke my pelvis. It banged me up pretty bad. The poles must have slid the full length of my back bone, on the side like. It left me black and blue down my back. Tough shape. That's the only time I blacked out.

The first time I was sent out to White Shoals was to remove the 300 mm lantern from the top of the tower. The lantern was all metal and weighed about 175 pounds. There was a metal ladder from the platform to the edge of the roof. It was quite a stretch from the edge of the lantern well. It was 125 feet above the water and there was nothing to fall on except concrete or water. It sure made me feel shaky, but we got it down just in time.

At about 5 o'clock that evening a storm set in blowing out of the northwest. I was sitting in a small office watching TV at about 10:30 p.m.. There was a hanging light in the ceiling. It seemed to me that out of the corner of my eye the light moved, but when I looked right at it I couldn't detect any movement. I began to feel a bit uneasy so I asked the chief if the tower shook. He said it does when we get a storm but not to worry because it had happened before and so far no damage had been done.

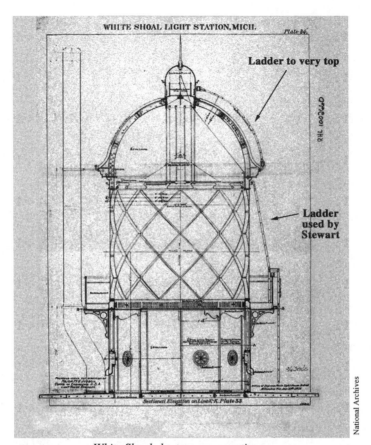

White Shoals lantern cross section

The snap shot of White Shoals is to show you where the winter light was located and that is where the flashing unit operating off acetylene gas was located. That knob on top of the tower was a 300 mm AGA buoy type light. We replaced this light later on with two 200mm AtoN lights operating off air cell batteries. These were used when the station closed for winter. We installed these lights on the decks, one on the left side for ships going to Chicago or to Burns Harbor and one on the right side of the hand rail for those going to northern Wisconsin. While we were up there a storm blew in fast, lightning etc. A flash hit the lead in to the radio equipment about 10 feet from us, knocked out the beacons but never touched us.

LAKE MICHIGAN

WHITE SHOALS LIGHT — 68

Stewart Edward

White Shoals had two passing 200mm lights on the north and east side on the outside railing

My last experience on White Shoal was not mechanical. In the lighthouse service most of the employees were in the 25 or older group. When the Coast Guard took over they put you with young fellows in the 18-19 year age group. Some of these couldn't stand the close confinement and isolation. This trip out we had a two week job to do so we stayed right there. One of those three or four day storms came in out of the northeast and one young lad couldn't take it. He started acting weird and put the rest of us on edge. He was a big young guy and there aren't many places to run on that light! The chief finally called the office. They couldn't send a boat out because they wouldn't be able to get close to the crib without getting damaged. The Traverse City Coast Guard Station finally agreed to come out with a helicopter. It sure was a relief when they came in sight and dropped a basket down and took the guy off.

I heard about people that went to a crib light and they rode up to the deck in a boat. Was that the usual procedure?
They had to lift the boat up anyway. If you wanted to wait and ride the boat up you could. You could walk up the ladder too.

Sweets Point

I heard it was tricky to hook the cable on the boat?
Yes, you had to know what you were doing right then because you didn't have a minute or two to think about whether to hook it. Talking about crib lights. The chief and I went out to Sweets Point to do something to the light. Of course there was a light attendant stationed at DeTour. He ran us out in his little 26-foot boat. We got out at the light. He tied up to the ladder there. It was kind of cool, it was in November. We got inside the tower and shut the door. There was no wind and it was alright. It took about 20 minutes, probably longer, about an hour I guess. When we came out there was the boat, way out there - too far for us to reach. If it hadn't been for a freighter going by . . . They called the Sault. They sent another boat out to get us.

DeTour

They are working on DeTour now.
Yes. Bruce Miller's dad was foreman when they built it originally. He is dead. It amazes me. The original cost of that light was only peanuts compared to what it is costing today.

We were lucky. Charlie Jones was the keeper while I was there. I forget the name of the assistants, two men from Duluth anyway. Charlie was a good cook. I don't know what I was doing out there. They were short on rooms so I slept on the couch. He didn't tell me they were going to blow the fog horn. Some time during the night the fog came in. The horn was right down underneath, on the side by the bunk. When that horn went off I must have jumped that high (two feet).

They had type F Diaphone fog horns. Power to them was supplied by Ingersoll Rand air compressors. Horns operated off of 40 pounds of air pressure. The compressors were single cylinder and had a blow torch attached to the cylinder head to preheat it. When the piston drove up, the hot head exploded the oil and drove the piston back. The compressor had two large fly wheels, about 5' in diameter, which were rotated by hand to get the compressor operating. It would fire once after about every three or four revolutions. Current for operating the station was supplied by a large 54 cell bank of batteries. Most aids to navigation equipment was in duplicate. There were two clocks, two compressors and two generators. Later on commercial power was supplied by submarine cable.

My first off-base job was to help the foreman when he had a job installing a new bank of batteries at DeTour. The battery bank was in the basement so he rigged up some line and we would hoist one battery up and let one down. The battery had to be handled by hand, carrying the old one outside and the new one in. I saw the foreman put on a rubber apron. My overalls began to get holes in the front from the acid off the old batteries. It was one lesson that I remembered when I was sent out later years to replace banks by myself.

Stewart's Lessons
Wear a rubber apron when handling wet cell batteries

Did you ever do anything at Poe Reef?
Oh yeah, I went to Poe Reef, Martins Reef, Spectacle Reef.

Did you know Ed Schmidt, keeper at Poe Reef?
I might of, I don't remember. That's when the log book would sure come in handy. The only things I changed on Fourteen-Foot Shoal were lamp changers. It had living quarters. They should have sold that. I've been on Martins too. There is not much to tell about them. Nothing happened.

Spectacle Reef

Spectacle Reef was about the most . . . It was like Stannard Rock. The Spectacle Reef lens was a Fresnel lens made of a large number of prisms which concentrated the light source to a central point. This was a second order lens and the only one like it that I ever worked on. It had 16 bulls eyes and revolved at one revolution per minute. It had a characteristic red and white flash. All the lenses were beautiful pieces of workmanship. During the late '60s and early '70s Spectacle Reef was being set up to be automated. We had received three small generators to operate the main light, and foghorn when needed. We had to bolt two generators to a concrete base and run fuel lines to each. They operated on diesel fuel. Overhead feeder lines were run from the generators to a three foot by five foot control panel. The generators operated on a 12 hour schedule and a clock on the panel would automatically switch engines. If one failed, a maintenance person would have to go replace the defective one and bring it into the shop for repairs.

The rooms were very small and were in the tower where the office and radio room were located. With the radio gear, a desk and some bookshelves it left just about room enough to turn around. A spiral stairway was constructed within the walls. The stairway was very narrow.

About a year before Spectacle Reef was slated for automation one of the civil engineers was sent up to the Soo to check it out for material, etc. He was about 6'4" and 190 pounds and hadn't been around many offshore lights. The floor of the lens room was 1/2 inch steel plate with a small trap door. Well, this fellow pushed the door up but it slipped and landed on his head and put a five inch cut in it. We couldn't stop the bleeding so we had to call Cheboygan and have them come out and take him to the hospital. It took quite a few stitches which didn't do much for his headache.

The next incident happened about a month after we installed the generators and started running AC circuits to the main light room, to the kitchen, water system and furnace. The officer in charge and I were working on a pump when all at once the generator started racing. Sparks started to fly and the officer in charge said, " Get out. She's going to blow up." He ran to get out of the building and all I could think of was to shut off the fuel supply which I did, but not soon enough to save the panel. He told me that somewhere in his past he had experienced the same problem and at that time the plant did explode. Seems funny the reactions of people to the same type of problems. It's a good thing we hadn't damaged any of the DC equipment because it took us the rest of the day to get the station back in operation again.

These November storms are out of this world. We were out there in '70, two of us, November 20th. Chief McEwan and I were on Specs putting in some new converter equipment. The first day wasn't too bad. It was rough getting to the light and we weren't sure we would be able to get onto the light. Waves were increasing in size and the wind was shifting around to the northeast with a few snow squalls. But after some good boat handling, we got off and our material with us. Along about dusk the waves started breaking over the crib and washing against the building. It wasn't safe to go out on deck. On one side of the engine room was a set of double doors for bad storms and also for when the light was closed for winter. The doors were equipped with steel shutters that could be closed from inside. A storm came up. The waves came in. We dropped down the steel doors, shut them. The waves would came in hard. We were sitting up in the wee office room. . .

Start of storm that put the light out.

There were three there besides us. You could almost feel the jolts. Around midnight everyone started calling in to tell us the light was out. The Soo was calling us, St. Ignace, Martin Reef, DeTour Reef were calling us. So I went up and the light was on. Spray from the waves plus snow and falling temperatures had coated the outside of the windows blocking the light. With winds getting up to 60 or more knots, it wasn't safe to go out onto the lantern deck. There was no way to get out there. None of us went to bed the second night. Water had started coming in over the main panel where the engine room was attached to the tower. We finally rigged a drip pan to keep the power panel dry. We had big propane tanks anchored on the side of the building outside. They had 1" bolts with strap iron around them into the building. We never did find them. Washed the deck clean. They were for our cooking. So we couldn't cook. We ate cold stuff. Corn beef and stuff. We did have heat. They kept calling. Our antenna had gone down on the radio system. Our TV was still working. Our chief said maybe we can switch antennas.

So we did. He took the lead from the TV to the radio. So we could tell them that we were alright.

The next day the storm quieted down so we could check the damage outside. We found the lines holding the radio antennae had broken insulators and the antennae collapsed. One end of a line was hanging over a ledge and frozen in ice. The chief grabbed the cable and gave it a yank to loosen it and when it broke loose the broken insulator slipped through his hand and cut a bad gash across his hand between his thumb and fingers. The best we could do to try and stop the bleeding was to take a piece of the broom handle, make a paste out of flour, put a thick patch of paste on the cut, lay the piece of broom on top of the paste and clench his fingers around it. Then we put a tight bandage around the hand. All we had for pain killers were aspirin. While we were fixing the chief's hand the officer in charge, LeLievre, was contacting St. Ignace which said even though the waves were running pretty high they would send a boat out. They got there all right but couldn't tie up. They pulled in a couple of times until the right wave came. It raised the boat up so the chief could jump in. Two crew men on the boat were there to catch him. It took ten stitches to close the wound.

Stewart Edward had a twinkle in his eye before he told each story

Richard L. Moehl

Gray's Reef

In late fall and early spring the winter light was set in place and operated off acetylene gas with a K-130 flasher. The station had a radiobeacon and air diaphone horns for fog and low visibility.

Were you around when the freighter hit Gray's Reef?
Oh yeah. They called us to check it. We drove down and then went out. The crew said the steamer reported the fog signal wasn't working. So when we figured we were 12 miles from the light we went slow. We shut the motor off and we could hear it. It was working, so we kept going. When the ship went by, her anchor had hit the corner of the crib. It chipped quite a chunk of cement off.

Nobody got hurt. It didn't do any serious damage. The accident knocked the ship's anchor off the bow of the ship and it was later recovered from the lake by the Coast Guard.

Miscellaneous

I never did get to Menagerie Island, Passage Island, no. I was at Bayfield. It's the only fog horn I ever changed. I never saw one like it. They sent me up there to put in a Wallace and Tiernan type fog horn. The one I took out had a ballast ringer with a gas operated engine. They had a bell. There was a cam, when they started the gas engine, there is an arm on the cam, like a hammer head. The cam would bring that up and then would drop it off and ring the bell. In all the bells I changed, and I changed quite a few, that's the only one I ever saw like that.

Did you see the bell on the Cheboygan Crib light?
We had eight of the bells that we brought in. When they started bringing them in I called the guy that runs the museum in the Soo. You should try to get one of those bells because they have US Lighthouse on them. We brought eight in. Somehow they turned them over to the college up there. Here about a year or so ago I called them and they said they don't have them.

Do you have any idea where any of the lenses went?
No, we brought in a lot of lens but I don't know where they went. You ought to go out to Spectacle Reef. The Coast Guard does maintenance. That is the most beautiful lens I ever saw. It's a round lens.

It has been taken out and is in Ohio.
That thing had 10 bulls-eyes, as I remember. Red and white, red and white. It is the only one I ever saw like it. Then there is no use going out there. The lens was the only good thing to see. Unless you want to climb that narrow stairway in the walls.

Poe Reef

I don't even want to get up on the crib.
Lordy, lordy. Poe Reef, I think it is. I was at Poe Reef in 1972 and I had one of those army belts with my tool kit on it. It happened to be Thanksgiving week during a month of bad storms. When I went out the new officer in charge had just moved in. He wasn't very acquainted with the area or the new type of boat the station had received, so he had his helper take me out in a new inboard-outboard motor boat. He said, "If the weather turns bad, you might have to spend

Thanksgiving on the light." Well, the storm moved in so I made up my mind to stay there; however, at about two o'clock Thanksgiving Day the helper called and said, "I'll be out to get you."

The new boat was small but easy to handle and it had lots of power. It could do up to forty miles per hour in good conditions. Coming alongside the light was pretty tricky with waves running four feet or so. It wasn't possible to tie up. He just had to jockey along the side. I was about halfway down the ladder and ready to jump when he came in on top of the wave. Well my belt slipped and hit the water. I looked around the water I couldn't see it. So I lost my belt.

I decided to retire in 1973. In the meantime, the Coast Guard gave one of four civilian workers, who was a scuba diver, a work order. He had to make the rounds of the lighthouses on concrete structures and inspect the underwater condition. Some were losing material washed out from under the steel plating. When he checked Poe Reef, the area near the ladders was partially washed out and he could see something shiny. When he reached in it was my tool kit, complete with tools. So, knowing I was going to retire the next spring, they cleaned things up and presented the tool kit to me at my retirement dinner. It sure was a pleasant surprise. I've got the tool kit yet.

Fourteen-Foot Shoal

Fourteen-Foot Shoal had a small kitchen, a bedroom, an office, and a machine room. During the 1960s a submarine cable was run out to the light to provide commercial power to the structure. A contractor had been given the job to install the cable at the light and wire up the light. Also, they had to mount a generator to provide power in the event that the shore line failed. It had most of the furnishings and aids to navigation equipment and lighthouse items: blankets, dishes, silverware, a brass wall clock, and also a brass barometer. Another Coast Guard took me along to install the new AC light and equipment. We were there three days while the other work was being done. A year later I was sent out in the spring to check the failure of the light to come on. I got there OK but the spring ice break-up had pulled two power cables out of the building. With no heat in the building, the starting batteries for the standby generator froze and busted. So I couldn't do much.

When I got back to the Cheboygan station the officer in charge told me that when the contractor completed his job on the light he stopped at the station and said, "Your clock and barometer are gone and I want you to know none of my men took them." So the chief called the guy who was with me and asked him about it.

Darn if he didn't blame me. The chief said if this isn't turned back, somebody will have to be turned in. He told me that two days later a package arrived from the Sault via UPS with no name or return address with the clock and barometer. In the meantime my partner had been transferred to Hawaii. I often wondered. So much of that stuff was left.

I did a lot of work on Marquette Harbor. Nice little town there. Crisp Point light. When I was out there, there was a double dwelling there. . . . If you walk from Whitefish Point to Crisp Point you will find streaks of sand, streaks of rough

Fourteen-Foot Shoal

rocks, then you will find another stretch of smaller stones. They are beautiful in the water.

In all my years of being in places to fish, the only place I ever fished was Huron Island. I caught a nice trout out from the boat house. Stannard Rock sets on the edge of a shoal. The tender can come in one area. This was a great area for lake trout. I remember being out there with Kane from the Soo. He was a good fisherman. I never saw such huge swarms of fish as I did there. He never caught any but I watched him. He would throw out his bait and the trout would follow it in but about the time they caught up, the hook would be out of the water. He never did get one. The keeper there set his own nets and sold to the commercial fishermen when they came in to pull up their nets.

Old Mackinac Point, I was there. The keeper there was Marken, he finally got killed. He transferred down to Northport or somewhere. He and his wife went out one night to a grange party or something. Coming home, it is a steep hill coming down into the light, right about the bottom there is a sharp turn. He didn't make the turn. Killed the woman and himself.

The only guy that I know that has a log book is the guy running Split Rock right now. I've been doing a lot of work with him. They sent another guy and me up there to bury a power cable to put in commercial current. Darn, there is no place to dig there. They brought all that stuff into the dock. To me that is a beautiful lighthouse. There are certain lighthouses that should have been kept: Spectacle Reef, Stannard Rock, Split Rock that are really important lights, even Pt. Iroquois.

The old lighthouse service wouldn't sell this stuff. They would take it out and dump it in the lake in the winter. The Coast Guard would take it out to the army garbage. All these flashers and stuff like that went to Kincheloe. I imagine that stuff was sold for scrap iron.

I liked those old fog horns I really did. Those old FT4s. Gall durn, I don't believe I ever heard the bells.

During my 37 years I had the chance to work with all senior men – Miller, Jones, Wilson plus the office sent me to Watertown, NY for six weeks to work with a civilian repairing AGA flashers and fog horn systems and then six weeks at the AtoN School in Groton, Conn. The only time I can recall having problems was when I didn't follow their advice.

Bruce taught me to keep your tools clean.

Stewart's Lessons
Keep your tools clean

Wilson taught me to cut and measure material when working with wood. I was helping and the lumber he was using had to be cut to size. I was cutting some 4 ft. boards and thought, why keep on measuring? I'll just use one for a pattern. He had to go to the shop for something and by the time he got back I had quite a few boards cut. He used a half dozen then he said, how are your measuring these boards, they don't fit? I told him what I did and he said use the rule each time you cut a board. With a pattern you change the length of your board. He was right.

Stewart's Lessons
Measure every time before you cut

Next was the electrician I went on jobs with as a helper. He said "keep one hand in your pocket." That meant just be careful around hot wires. He also said, if you are in an area where other folks are around and you are working on hot lines close the panel and lock it. Every problem I had was when I didn't remember to be careful and follow this advice.

Stewart's Lessons
Always keep one hand in your pocket

DeTour Reef was having a problem with power from the commercial line and sent me and a 3rd class electrician down to check it out. We went to the case where their power came in to the transformers. I asked the chief how much voltage they had coming in (my first mistake). He said 440. I started to get up to stand where the transformers were and the young lad said, "I'll do that. You stand here on the rubber mat." I did. He took the end of the leads. I held the meter. He got one lead on and when he reached to put the other lead there was a loud crack and my meter disintegrated. I don't know how we weren't electrocuted. Then I checked and there was 2,700 volts coming in. Some mistake! I still didn't learn. . .

Next I was sent to Copper Harbor to change bulbs in a 36" aerobeacon. I think that was when they increased the wattage from 500 to 1,000. Well my helper couldn't climb towers – the ladders were on the outside and the tower is around

100'. I said, "OK, shut the switch off" (my second mistake). I got to the top no problem. But when I opened the front of the beacon I couldn't reach in to the changer so I stood on the railing, held the door open, and reached in. When my other hand hit the lamp changer I got a jolt through both arms and nearly fell off the tower. I let out a yell. He said he had turned the switch off. When I got down I looked and there were two circuits, one for commercial power and one for the battery-operated standby light. He turned off the battery light. Again, no one to blame but myself.

One more place to show how I made problems by not using books of instruction on a repair problem. Late on a weekend a chief bosun mate and I were sent to an offshore light in Lake Michigan to replace a faulty generator. We took one we had in the shop and a tender took us out. We just had to replace the one set up with the one we brought. It was late when we were just about completed and the tender was ready to leave. A storm was coming up. Something was wrong and the one we took didn't work out either. The tender finally said we are leaving in an hour. I couldn't figure out what was wrong so we put the old one back on the line. I said if you're not staying I'm not either. We took off and while having coffee in the mess deck, I looked through the instruction book and there was the answer to my problem. An electric chief had told me a year before that books of instruction come with all equipment. The problem was the generators could be hooked up for 220 or110 and somewhere our generator had been turned to 110. When I hooked it up the panel wouldn't work. If I only had read the directions! All I had to do was change one wire.

Stewart's Lessons
Read the instructions

Round Island

This light got to be a meeting place for some young folks who had boats and held parties there. I can't recall if it was in the '50s or '60s that Hubert Rogers, a civilian diver and marine construction man, got orders from our Cleveland office to go out and knock the building down. He bought dynamite and caps to do the job. When news got around about what was going to happen, a group of folks got together and with the help of politicians got the group permission to restore the light for a museum.

Martin Reef

This was another one of the lights where I did wrong. This was in the shad fly season and I was changing some standby equipment from acetylene to battery operation. Those structures got pretty warm inside in the summer time due to windows being steel frames and no screens. Most of the time we would give the fellow on watch a hand with washing dishes. Well, he was in the little office doing some paper work. It was after dark so when I got done I opened the windows in the kitchen and went into the next room and turned on a light. It wasn't too long before I knew why the windows weren't open. That light drew shad flies in by the hundreds. By the time I figured out where they were coming from the kitchen was a mess!

In the lighthouse days the main keeper was in charge and then you had two or three assistant keepers depending on the importance of your light. Well, the keeper made up the meals, did book work, and took care of reports. We always got a good meal. However when the Coast Guard took over, the man on watch in the morning got breakfast; whoever was on watch at mealtime made the meal. We had a surprise one morning out at Martins Reef after the Coast Guard took over. Some young "Coastie" had his first time to cook and he served us chili. Sure was hot! One night two of us were up in the Lake Superior area, we landed at the light at about 5 p.m. and they fed us bologna sandwiches and potato chips for supper. Later that night after we had all turned in we thought we smelled steaks being cooked. Things got better the next day.

Martin Reef Light before a storm

Richard L. Moehl

Split Rock

In 1965 two of us from Soo Base were sent to Split Rock to lay an underground cable to the two dwellings to supply standby power in case commercial power failed. At that time commercial power was not in the light tower. Water was pumped from a pump house located about 800 feet from the dwellings into a large storage tank that supplied the dwelling. Later on, a well was drilled through solid rock at an angle into Lake Superior.

Was the Soo always your base?
Well, Uncle Sam took me away for a year. They couldn't get along without me. The Coast Guard didn't want me with a uniform on. They gave me a furlough to go. As soon as I got out I came back to the Soo.

You liked the lighthouse service?
Absolutely! It was for me.

Why?
There is something about it. Even isolated lights. I felt right at home in them. I liked to go up there at night and watch the birds flying around.

Do you think you might have liked being a keeper?
I'd liked to have been a keeper, yeah. But traveling was alright too.

Was there a lot of creativity involved?
We were never in want of anything. We also had meals. We didn't have to cook. We had a little discussion. . . I really liked it.

STANNARD ROCK LIGHT
LAKE SUPERIOR

Stewart Edward

Stannard Rock from bow of boat in some swells

FM GRU Charlevoix
To CGGONine
Info CGBase Soo
Zen/CGC Sundew

Lansing Shoals Report of Storm Damage

1. Winds of 60 plus kts. and seas of 15-20 feet battering the east side of subject station for period of 8 to 10 hours caused heavy damage to structure and equipment. Crew has been evacuated to Charlevoix by CGC Sundew. No serious injuries sustained by crew. Following is reported damaged.

A. Structure
   1. 5 broken ports beyond repair
   2. bulkhead between northern double ports on east side was observed working in heavy seas
   3. cracks over all of inside east bulkhead of engine room
   4. south east corner and lower east wall concrete seriously sluffed off
   5. north east end of railing missing
   6. storm ports glass cracked in at least two additional ports
   7. inside overhead on main deck cracked from cascading waves breaking on second deck
   8. all concrete blocks on main deck covering blown or mashed away over all of east side and half of north side. Five blocks were found inside engine room
   9. coal scuttle hatch over fuel oil room missing and fuel oil room open to elements
   10. three 2000 pound concrete sinkers located on east side against superstructure and used for boom test were shifted about main deck and was displaced to opposite of crib
   11. all storm windows along main deck on east side destroyed
   12. one broken pane in main light lantern room
   13. all storm windows on east side of tower cracked or broken

B. Machinery
   1. fuel oil day tank gauge broken and tank flooded
   2. both generators submerged
   3. both generator engines have water internally throughout
   4. both compressor engines have water internally throughout
   5. furnace boiler and blower were completely submerged
   6. water pump motor submerged

C. Electronics
   1. radio beacon transmitters completely inundated by solid streams of water
   2. master clocks submerged with external damage to at least one
   3. f/m converter wetted but was useable prior to evacuation
   4. both 649 receivers antenna broken
   5. TV antennae, booster and rotor carried away

2. Unit is considered uninhabitable without major repairs. Request structural engineer to conduct on site survey of damage. Recommend electrical conversion to alternating current power using generators previously destined for automation of Spectacle Reef and presently located at Cheboygan. Recommend all radio beacon equipment be removed and completely overhauled and reinstalled in new location in watch room as planned.

Stewart was sent to repair Lansing Shoal after this 1970 storm

UNITED STATES COAST GUARD

CONTRACT NO. Tcg-39293

1 July, 1953 to 30 June, 1954

ELECTRIC MARINE BEACONS

LANTERNS
LAMPCHANGERS
FLASHER MECHANISMS
BATTERY CANS

WALLACE & TIERNAN COMPANY, INC.
BELLEVILLE 9, N. J.

Printed in U.S.A.

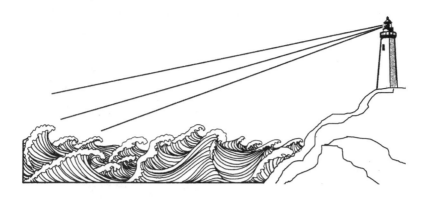

Radiobeacon

Radiobeacons were essentially AM radio transmitters used during foggy weather in much the same way as fog signals. Each radiobeacon-equipped lighthouse or light vessel transmitted a series of repeated Morse code signals unique to that station, in much the same way as each station exhibited a unique light and fog signal pattern to readily identify the station. These were all referred to as the station's characteristic.

Vessels capable of navigating using the radiobeacon signals were outfitted with a specific type of radio receiver with an antenna which could be rotated until the strength of the signal was found to be at its minimum level. Such a receiver was known as a radiocompass since it would point directly to the source of the radiobeacon transmission in much the same way as a regular compass points to magnetic north.

Once the exact directions of two or three radiobeacon's transmissions were identified, a mariner could triangulate and hence plot his location in relation to the known points of origin of the signals.

Radiobeacons at many stations were controlled to transmit their radio signal at the exact second that an audible signal was sounded. The radio signal travels so fast that you receive it essentially instantaneously. However the audible signal travels slowly, at the pace of one mile every five seconds. Thus the ship's captain could calculate his distance from the source by counting the seconds between receiving a radiobeacon and hearing the audible signal, then dividing by five to get the number of miles distant. The Coast Guard says the error from such a calculation will not exceed 10 percent.

The Lighthouse Service undertook its first radiobeacon tests at the Navesink Light Station in New Jersey in 1917. The first radiobeacon on the Great Lakes was installed onboard the Lake Huron Lightship in 1925. By 1931 there were 33 radiobeacon stations throughout the Great Lakes.

The radiobeacon system was largely rendered obsolete by the adoption of RADAR and LORAN systems in the 1940's.

- Terry Pepper

The Mariner

U. S. Lighthouse Service 1936, thanks to Terry Pepper

This system worked because of the cooperative efforts of the mariner and the lighthouse keeper. The mariner had a radiocompass on his boat that would give a plot towards all radiobeacons operating within range of the boat. Identifying the direction of each signal was known as "taking the minimum."

The Lighthouse

The mariner would tune in a certain kilocycle identified on the Light List as being used by lighthouses in the vicinity. If you were approaching Duluth in 1951 using the chart below you would tune in to 308 kilocycles in the 2nd and 5th 10 minute sounding interval as shown on the clock. You would listen for the three different morse codes being transmitted at the west end of Lake Superior. For the first minute Duluth would be sounding dash, dash dash, dot. Then Superior Entry would sound dash, dot, dot for one minute and then Two Harbors would sound dot, dash, dash, dot. This set of signals would repeat three times in the 10 minute block and then there would be one minute of silence. These stations would begin to broadcast again in the 5th time period, i.e. 40 minutes before the hour.

Characteristic code is given by dots and dashes followed by frequency in kilocycles

Sequence of operation within a goup is indicated by Roman numeral before name (Ex. II)

The scheduled 10 minute period of clear weather transmisssion during each hour is given in brackets after name [2-5]. See clock face. The last minute of each 10 minute clear weather period is silent.

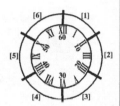

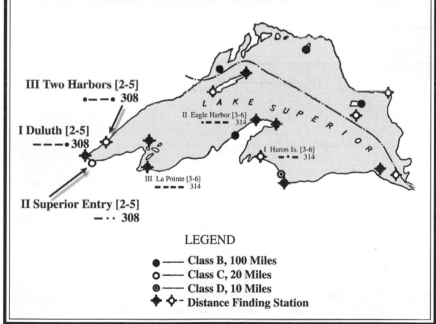

III Two Harbors [2-5]
•— —• 308

I Duluth [2-5]
— — —• 308

II Superior Entry [2-5]
— •• 308

II Eagle Harbor [3-6]
•— —• 314

I Huron Is. [3-6]
— •— 314

III La Pointe [3-6]
— — —• 314

LEGEND

● —— **Class B, 100 Miles**
○ —— **Class C, 20 Miles**
◉ —— **Class D, 10 Miles**
✦ ◇ - **Distance Finding Station**

The Plot

The mariner plots three different signals with his radiocompass and determines that they are coming from the directions shown at left.

From his chart he identifies the lighthouse sending each different Morse code and replots his lines on the chart as shown. He now knows that his boat lies within the triangle created by the intersection of these lines. The more precise his readings the smaller the triangle and hence the more exactly he knows his location.

III Two Harbors [2-5]
•━ ━• 308

I Duluth [2-5]
━ ━ ━• 308

II Superior Entry [2-5]
━ • • 308

Distance Finding Station

Two Harbors and Duluth are also distance finding stations. Because radiowaves and sound waves travel at different speeds it is possible for the mariner to time the interval between receiving the radio signal and hearing an audible bell. He can take this time lag and convert it into miles distant. Thus one distance finding station provides enough information for the mariner to locate his boat.

Boat hears signal 50 seconds after receiving radiobeacon.

Thus boat is 10 miles from Duluth Station.

I Duluth [2-5]
━ ━ ━• 308

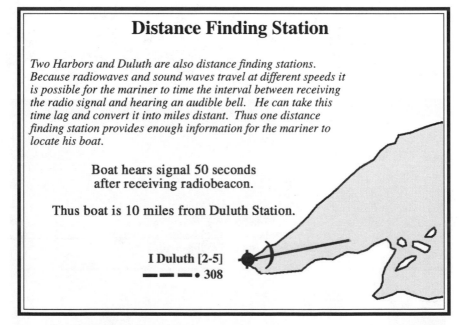

2

Bill Muessel

Served from 1939 to 1973

Interviewed June 2nd, 2002 by Terry Pepper

Bill Muessel served from 1939 to 1973, roughly the same period as Stewart Edward, but his memories differ. Bill had the option of becoming a Coast Guardsman when the Lighthouse Service was abolished, and he took it. This gave him different job options plus the military obligations imposed when the Coast Guard was subsumed by the Navy during WWII.

Bill was both a lighthouse tender crewman and a lighthouse keeper. He spent considerably more time away from home than Stewart and his memories reflect the concerns resulting from this separation from his family.

The risks of lighthouse service come up several times in Bill's memories. A shipmate killed in service, fellow keepers lost in a boat on Lake Superior, and the wreck of the Cox just offshore of Rock of Ages are still on Bill's mind 60 years later.

Separation from family is also a poignant memory. The stolen moments with his wife and children while serving on Rock of Ages and the loving care he put into improving their improvised rendezvous cabin expose his *concern about their family time while he was stationed on an offshore lighthouse three weeks out of four.*

Bill also points to the most important management concern regarding the offshore service at an all electric lighthouse - keeping busy. As lighthouse duty transformed itself from the under-manned era of the 1800s into the Coast Guard's over-manned stations of the 1900s, it was difficult to find adequate work to keep crewmen's minds off their lonely plight on remote stations. The modern equipment took far less work than the kerosene-fueled equipment. As head keeper, Bill kept his crew busy with painting the massive tower. But he also acknowledges the importance of fishing to fill the time and provide a tasty source of fresh food.

Despite the concerns and hardships, Bill stayed with the service for 34 years and 6 months.

Bill, please tell me where you grew up and how you became involved with Rock of Ages Light.
I was born in 1918, hard on the shores of Lake Superior on Park Point in Duluth, Minnesota. I was involved in sailing on Lake Superior for many years and with the lighthouses in various positions in Lake Superior.

My first trip to Rock of Ages was in 1939. I joined the Lighthouse Service in early spring of 1939 and the Coast Guard took over the former Lighthouse Service in 1940. At that time I enlisted in the Coast Guard. I remained in the Coast Guard for 34 years and retired in the fall of 1973, after 34 years and six months of service. When I retired I was the last person that came from the Lighthouse Service in enlistment status. I had a lighthouse pennant that flew from the buoy tenders. I was in Castle Hill, Rhode Island when I retired. We hoisted the Lighthouse Service pennant at that time, they hauled it down, and they presented it to me.

Amaranth
1939-1942

When I first made a trip out to Rock of Ages in 1939, I was on the *Amaranth*, a 180-foot buoy tender which worked out of Duluth. It was a coal-burning steam vessel with a crew of 28. We were all civilians, members of the Lighthouse Service. Our main job as a tender was to bring supplies, machinery, maintenance men and workers out to the lighthouses. We mainly worked Lake Superior; however, occasionally we would go below the Soo. I was on the *Amaranth* from about March of 1939 until November of 1942, shortly after Pearl Harbor, when I was transferred off the buoy tender and went other places.

I think it was during the first year that I was on the *Amaranth*, in 1939, when we delivered a new air compressor to Rock of Ages and we picked up the old air compressor. It was a nice quiet day. We had a scow that we hoisted aboard the buoy tender and when we got to the lighthouse we would hoist the scow (a small barge) with the boom into the water and put coal, machinery or oil barrels, or whatever we might have on it.

Ontonagon County Historical Society,
Ontonagon, Michigan

The Amaranth *sitting at the Duluth South Breakwater with the lighthouse in the background. For scale see the man waving at the front of the pilot house.*

Bill, how long would you say that scow was?
I think it was not more than 30 feet. Not more than 30 by 15. We'd tow the scow with a gas launch that we also had on the *Amaranth*. We were bringing this old Fairbanks Morse compressor back. It was on a steel base. When we came alongside the buoy tender the first mate was on the scow and the second mate was running the launch that was towing the scow. They came alongside rather vigorously and with somewhat of an impact, and it caused the air compressor to start sliding. The steel base of the compressor sat on the steel deck of the scow, we didn't have any dunnage under it. The compressor started sliding inboard toward the tender. We were alongside the tender at this time and it caused the scow to upend. We had some empty oil barrels and some other stuff, and things were flying around. One of the deck hands, Sunny Burgmarker from Duluth, tried to pull himself up into the gangway of the *Amaranth* when the scow caught him in the hips as it flipped, and crushed him. They got him aboard and after we got the scow and everything stowed, the skipper, Patty O'Donnell, headed for Houghton, which was the closest place with hospital facilities. He really cranked her up. The coal-passers were throwing coal and we had a full head on, but it still took us several hours to get to Houghton. By the time we got Sunny to the hospital he had expired. A couple of the other guys also were hurt, but not too seriously.

We used to bring the lighthouse keepers out in the spring. On Lake Superior, when she'd freeze up, they would close down all the lights and navigation would cease. In December, sometime around Christmas, we'd bring the lighthouse keepers in. Then in the spring, about March or the early part of April, we'd take them back out. We'd also bring their supplies out at that time. During the summer season the tenders worked buoys and other aids to navigation including lighthouses.

As far as Rock of Ages was concerned, the keepers were all civilians at that time. They'd usually have a keeper and three assistants: a third, second and first assistant. At that time I never had any suspicion that I would end up stationed on Rock of Ages. After leaving the *Amaranth* in 1942, I went to Detroit and other places on the lakes, and was transferred to the East Coast. After the war, I came back to the lakes and I was assigned to a buoy tender in Lake Michigan, the *Tamarack*. At that time she was being used primarily to tend diving bells that the Navy was developing. We had a huge bell that we'd keep in the hold. We'd pick it up with the boom and drop it into the water. They'd put divers down and practice with the diving bell.

I left the *Tamarack* in '46. I was only on it for about a year, and I came back to Group Duluth. I went to Outer Island where I was stationed for about half the season. The keeper was a civilian, and I was able to bring my wife out there and

Riuchard L. Moehl

Outer Island with the staircase from the water up the cliff shown at the very left.

one child at the time. We'd go back and forth in the gasoline launch. Outer Island is on the outside and there's not much protection there. On the backside we had a boat house and kind of a little harbor. On the front side we just had a dock down at the foot of the cliff. I made a kind of little fish box that we used to carry our baby in. The baby was less than a year old at the time. My wife always said that there were 93 steps coming up from the dock to the light. We had electricity to run the main light, but in the dwelling there was still kerosene. But we'd run an extension cord from the fog signal so we'd at least have some electricity. We had to clean the mantles in the kerosene lamps. I only stayed at Outer Island through that fall and returned to Duluth for the winter.

The following spring, I went out to Passage Island for part of the season until I was assigned to the Aids to Navigation School in Groton, Connecticut. I went to Groton in November of '48, and graduated out of the AtoN, Aids to Navigation, class in April of '49. Then I came back to Duluth Group and was assigned as the officer in charge of Rock of Ages.

Rock of Ages
1949-1954

I went out to Rock of Ages in June of 1949. I had been acquainted with the keeper since during the war he was a Lieutenant in the Coast Guard and was commanding officer of one of the tenders I was on in Lake Huron. The keeper was a civilian

ROCK OF AGES LIGHTHOUSE—ISLE ROYALE, LAKE SUPERIOR

Crane ———

——— Stairs to rock

Dock

Path to water

Post card from the files of John Tregembo

The crane above the dock was used to lift the boat up onto the deck. Two radiobeacon antennae served Rock of Ages (one to the left of the tower and the other at the right end of the Rock).

named Hubert Veislaw. I don't know how long he had been at Rock of Ages before I relieved him, but I would think that he was probably there two or three years, after discharge from the Coast Guard after the war. I was a boatswain's mate chief then, with a designator AtoN from graduating from the Aids to Navigation School. I was assigned as the officer in charge. I remained there until August of 1954, when I was transferred to Kodiak, Alaska, to a buoy tender up there.

So I was there a little more than five years. I enjoyed the tour of duty. They had some difficulty in finding people who were willing to stay on this isolated station for any length of time.

Especially married people, I would think.
Yes, that's right. You were out for three weeks and in for one week.

Where did your wife live when you were stationed out there?
She lived in Duluth all this time. While I was on there we used to run our liberty (boat) from Grand Portage, Minnesota, which is up by the Canadian border. There's

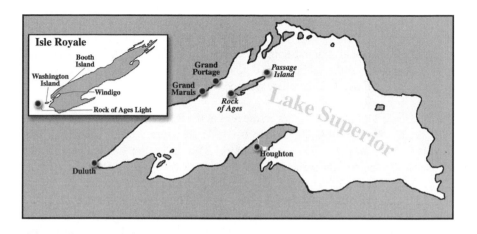

a little harbor there and that's where the mail boat and the fish boat came from to service Isle Royale. It was about nineteen miles across from Rock of Ages to Grand Portage. We used to run that in a 24-foot boat with usually two guys in the boat, one guy going ashore on liberty and another guy coming back from liberty. While I was at Rock of Ages we were under the Coast Guard Group at Grand Marais, which is maybe fifteen miles from Grand Portage, and that's where they'd send the truck with our supplies.

Then our supplies would be shipped out on one of several mail boats. They were gas boats which ranged from 40 to 60 feet. They would come out and make the whole run around Isle Royale, pick up the fish, trout and herring, and ice it down, and then bring it in to Grand Portage. In turn, they'd bring the supplies out to the fishermen and to Rock of Ages and Passage Island, being at the other end of Isle Royale. We would have to take our 24-footer with a 4-cylinder Gray engine and run into Washington Harbor from Rock of Ages. If we weren't there when the fish boat came through, they'd leave our supplies and mail in boxes in a fish shed in the harbor. It was kind of a derelict fish shed, but it held off the elements and we'd pick up our stuff there.

At Rock of Ages there is only a small cement dock, maybe 30 feet in length, and it really doesn't get any lee. We'd pick the boat up with a crane and set it on the second deck of the lighthouse. For some years, if the weather was such that you couldn't land at the Rock, you could tie-up at a little shack on Booth Island, which is right across from Singers Island in Washington Harbor. We kept some supplies and a bed there. I did quite a bit of improving on the cabin. I got a little gas generator so we could generate some electricity so we had lights. My wife would come out and stay at the cabin, and I'd go out there when I was available. We had two boys at the time. Our daughter was too small to take.

We used to do a lot of trout fishing on the reef at the Rock. The fishing was tremendous there. We got all kinds of lake trout. There were a lot of moose on Isle Royale. There still are. They were taboo. They'd let the Indians harvest the moose in the fall to thin them out, but they never really got many takers on it. They say the moose got to Isle Royale from the Canadian shore around 1910 when they had a severe winter and the lake iced over. There were no predators on the island so the moose kept expanding. At Windigo they had an area, a couple of acres, fenced off to keep the moose out so you could see how the vegetation grew where the moose couldn't get at it. They're like deer and eat everything as high as they can reach with their heads.

I always used to tell the crew that when coming back from Grand Portage if it was foggy you run two hours and, if you don't see the light, then you should stop and shut off the engine and listen for the horn. One time, when I was on a week's leave, a couple of non-rated guys, I think it was a fireman and a seaman, were running back to Rock of Ages from Grand Portage and forgot to stop and listen. They just kept motoring along until they ran out of fuel. A steamer came along and put a line on them and towed them as far as the Keweenaw Peninsula and called the Portage Coast Guard Station. The crew from Portage Station came out and escorted them back to the Rock. As I said, I was on leave and didn't know this until I got back.

When I was at the station for those five years you could still see the *Cox* (a famous shipwreck) about four feet under water, but she kept sliding down a little more every year. The first couple of years that she was exposed the fishermen were really in fat city. They were getting furniture in their fishing nets. I even heard a story that one of them pulled up a piano, but I don't know if that was true or not. At any rate, it was really good picking for them for a couple of years.

When you were stationed on Rock of Ages, what do you remember most about the inside of the structure?
The first two stories are inside the crib itself. They are steel. Then on top of the second deck, the brick lighthouse itself starts, about eight stories high. In the spring, when you would go out there, after sitting through the winter, it would take

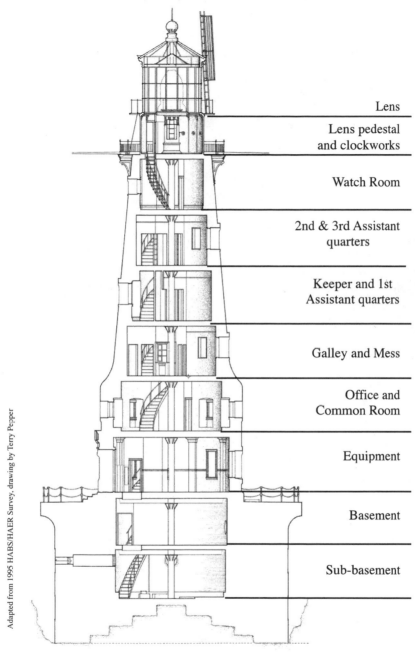

Lens

Lens pedestal
and clockworks

Watch Room

2nd & 3rd Assistant
quarters

Keeper and 1st
Assistant quarters

Galley and Mess

Office and
Common Room

Equipment

Basement

Sub-basement

Adapted from 1995 HABS/HAER Survey, drawing by Terry Pepper

Rock of Ages interior. The rooms are circular and smaller at each higher level. The stairs are on the outside of each floor. It does NOT have a center spiral staircase. The central tube was for the weight of the clock works. Uses of each floor varied over the years as the technology changed. For example, when the light was electrified the watch room was moved from near the light to near the generators.

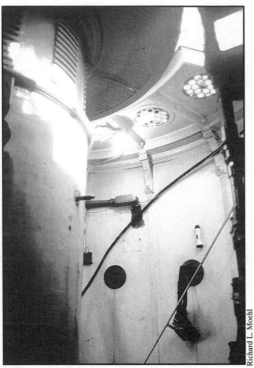

The clockworks room at Rock of Ages, looking up through the floor lights towards the lantern

about a week to warm the place up. We did have a furnace. It was coal fired to start with, but then they converted it to oil.

Was that hot water heat?
Yes, it was hot water with radiators. The first floor was the engine room, with the compressors, generators and the radio equipment, and that was where you stood your watch. The radiobeacons and the timers were all there. The next deck up was the galley and that's where the officer in charge had his bunk. The third, fourth and fifth decks also had bunks, and as you progressed up, the rooms got smaller. The lantern room was really two floors devoted to the light itself. Originally, they used to have weights that ran down five stories through a tube that ran down through the center. You would crank it up from the top side. The power to turn the light came from this weight through a clockwork mechanism. The light floated in mercury and that's what made the thing run so free and easily. We had shades in the lantern that we pulled every morning. We'd put a cover over the lens which we took off every night when we'd light her up. Of course, everything was electrified when I was there. But there was still a lot of the old equipment in there.

What type of thing did you do to pass the time, did you play a lot of cards or did you have a radio?
Before I got there I don't think there was too much work performed. But down in the lower crib deck there was a lot of block and tackle. They used to paint the light themselves, but it hadn't been done for many years before I got there. I had this guy, Ed Heinsberg, who'd been there for probably fifteen years before I got there because he was there when the *Cox* went down in '33. He was a Latvian from

Richard L. Moehl

Rock of Ages Light looms over the photographer. The first two floors, which have a larger diameter than above, are steel plated on the outside. The higher portion of the tower is plastered-over brick.

Riga, Latvia, and he had been a square-rigger sailor, sailing around The Horn many times. We got the block and tackle out and rigged it up from the lantern room and started scraping and painting on the light, which was a project that would take years. Down below the lower two levels were steel, and we had to do a lot of chipping because there was a lot of rust. The bricks were not so bad. I found out the best way to keep the crew happy was to keep them busy. However, we had a lot of time for trolling. Fishing was really the big thing. We had the radio. I had a couple of hillbilly kids and every Saturday night they had to listen to the Grand Old Opry.

I used to do a lot of trout fishing on Isle Royale itself. There were some really dandy trout streams there, and down at the bottom of Washington Harbor, at Windigo Lodge, they had a little dock, and that's where I would go trout fishing.

What bait would you use?
Mostly worms. It was pretty well overgrown, and they weren't the type of streams you could get a boat into. Once in awhile, you'd come across a wide spot, but that was about it. It was very good trout fishing.

Going back to your time on the Amaranth, *what were the quarters like on that vessel? She's long gone, and I have often wondered what life was like on board.*
The *Amaranth* was the first and last boat I was ever on that had a forecastle. The crew had quarters down in the forecastle, just back of the chain locker. It was maybe 25 or 30 feet long, but it wasn't beamy because you were up in the forward part of the vessel. Along the starboard and port sides we had six bunks, three fore and three aft, two deep, so we had a total of twelve bunks there.

We had seven deck hands and normally carried three coal-passers. Then we had a guy we called "the flunky." He was the helper in the galley. The second cook also lived in the forecastle. We had a wooden ladder we came down. It was almost vertical but had a little angle on it. There was a little table in the middle of the cabin. We used to play a lot of poker on it, but you couldn't seat more than four people at it comfortably.

As I said, as well as the three coal-passers, we normally had three firemen, three oilers and two engineers, the chief engineer and the first assistant engineer. That made up the engine room. Then on the deck division we had the seven deck hands and three quartermasters. The quartermasters would do all the wheeling, they'd go four and eight. Then when we'd stop at a lighthouse or work buoys, they would work the boom, because there'd be nobody in the wheel house, except probably

Richard L. Moehl

Jim Woodward standing on the deck at bulls-eye level on the Rock of Ages second order lens. This photo was taken during the lens removal from Rock of Ages in 1985.

the old man or the watch-stander. Then we had the first and second mate and the captain.

We also had a radio operator. In those days it was all "ditty-dot," you know, so we had "Sparky." There was also a steward who ordered all of the grub and kind of took care of the officers. Finally, there were the first and second cook and the flunky, so there was a total of three guys in the galley.

We didn't have any yeomen like they do now. There were no real administrative guys on board because we didn't really go through the paperwork like they do today.

In reading through various station log books, I have noticed that the Amaranth *and* Marigold *frequently carried various dignitaries and passengers on board. Were there staterooms on board for visitors?*
Yes. The Captain had his own quarters underneath the wheelhouse. The mate, second engineer and steward slept back on the aft upper deck. They had a salon back there, along with the officers mess, and that's where the inspector or any visitors would stay.

I also notice in station logs that the tenders frequently arrived very late and de-parted early. Is that the way things went when you were on her? Was she pretty much sailing all the time?
The weather would be the big factor. If we got there and the weather forecast looked good, we'd frequently make an early start, around four in the morning. We didn't really do too much midnight stuff, but we were mostly servicing the lights outside. Are you familiar with the *Marigold* at all?

I have read quite a bit about her. She was sold off, converted into a sand-sucker and worked the Saginaw River. She was the last of the old tenders to be scrapped about ten years ago.
She worked out of Detroit. We always did our dry-docking in Lake Michigan, Manitowoc mostly, or Sturgeon Bay. When we were out, then the *Marigold* would come up to Lake Superior, and vice versa.

Did you work out of the buoy depot on Minnesota Point?
No. When I was on the *Amaranth*, we were on Lake Avenue, just above the aerial bridge towards town. We had a sand lot that we'd throw the buoys in and that's where we'd paint them up in the spring. We were working with acetylene gas, that was before batteries, and we had those huge lanterns on the buoys.

How did they transfer the gas from the tender to the buoys? Did she have a large storage tank on board?

No, the gas was always in tanks. We'd get the acetylene in tanks, about three or four feet long, and maybe a foot or two in circumference. They'd weigh about 150 to 180 pounds, the big ones. They were the same as you see oxygen and acetylene in today when you see a guy doing some burning. They had some small tanks, but most of the buoys took these large tanks. I think they called them A-300's or something like that.

I had read some accounts of tanks being installed in the tenders to hold gas, and it was transferred by some type of hose. I did not know that you used tanks.

I think that maybe in the old, old days before they had these portable tanks, they had some buoys that had a big pocket in them, and they did pump the gas into them.

I always thought that would be a dangerous thing to be doing.

Yes. Most of our buoys were two-pocket buoys, some of them were three. You'd have to open the dogs on the pocket. (The latches that held the top tightly in place.) Then with the boom you'd pick the old tank out and drop a new one in. From there the gas was piped up to the lantern. The buoy had a diaphragm in there that would get the different characteristics out. You could adjust this diaphragm to make it quick flashing or interrupted, slow flashing, or whatever you wanted to do with it.

The Amaranth

Amaranth

Lighthouse Tender 1891-1945

As the final decade of the nineteenth century dawned the Lighthouse Board found itself hard pressed to keep up with construction, supply and inspection of the growing number of lighthouses in the Ninth and Eleventh Districts. Perhaps more importantly, the Ninth District headquarters were located on the Chicago waterfront, and with the Columbian Exhibition slated to be held in Chicago in 1893, the world would be coming to Chicago. The Lighthouse Board was scheduled to participate with a large display; a new tender would serve as a showpiece.

Designed as a schooner-rigged vessel with a wooden hull, twin coal-fired boilers and twin screws, the *Amaranth* was launched in 1891.

Progressive design features, including a large forward hold for cargo, drinking water, and ballast, as well as modern crew quarters including toilets and electric lights, allowed the *Amaranth* to serve until 1954. In addition, she pressed along at an impressive 14 miles per hour. She carried fore and aft steam capstans for loading and unloading supplies plus a 10-ton hoist for lifting buoys. She was versatile, modern and fast.

In 1900 the tender's decks were revamped and she was transferred to the Navy for service in WWI. However, the work didn't change; she continued carrying supplies to lighthouses and performing buoy maintenance.

With transfer of lighthouse duties from the Lighthouse Board to the Coast Guard in 1939, the *Amaranth* was given the Coast Guard designation WAGL-201. She served the Coast Guard through WWII, was decommissioned in the fall of 1945 and sold to a private owner in 1946. She then was re-powered with diesel engines and operated until 1954.

-Terry Pepper

3

Dick Campbell

Son of Keeper John P. Campbell

Served from 1932 - 1963

Interviewed on Dec. 8, 2003 by Sandy Planisek and Dick Moehl

The interview with Dick Campbell is the first of four interviews of children who lived on Huron Island in Lake Superior with their lighthouse keeper parents. Their stories concentrate less on the duties and occupations of lighthouse keepers and more on the family life of these keepers.

Dick's father, John Campbell, was keeper at four lighthouses: Grassy Island, Huron Island, Old Mackinac Point, and Point Betsie. Dick grew up at the first three of these. By the time his father moved to Point Betsie Dick was an adult and remained behind. We interviewed Dick in his Mackinaw City home. His wife, Nancy, helped answer questions. Her father, Elton Dagwell, was the marine reporter in Mackinaw and so it probably was logical that these two children would have a lot in common, enough to make a long, successful marriage.

Dick's memories start when he was a toddler at Grassy Island. Even though very young, he was allowed to go along on the buoy maintenance runs which seemed to constitute the majority of the work done by the keepers at Grassy Island. This, John's first lighthouse, was the start of a long family adventure in lighthouse service.

Huron Island was the lighthouse that left a life-long imprint on Dick.
Eight summers of roaming a rock island, with seven or eight other kids,
forced him and his playmates to invent games. They mimicked the
adults in fishing and helping with chores. They learned from the
adults, the few visitors, and from their inner creativity.

As you look over the pictures you will see that the island consists of a
huge rock topped with huge boulders. Walking on the trails was
dangerous because the planks got slippery. Walking off the trails was
never done by the adults and was a danger to the kids, even in their
tennis shoes.

When asked about chores, Dick talked about carrying water. The
Huron Island Lighthouse is about 170 feet above the water level.
Every drop of water used for drinking or cooking had to be carried up
that 170 feet, the equivalent of a 17 story building. Since water weighs
8.3 pounds per gallon, even the little kids, carrying two gallons, were
carrying over 16 pounds each trip to the top. The lighthouse service
apparently did not care about this huge inconvenience. Improvements
to the island included installing electric lines and fuel-oil pipes up to
the lighthouse, but never water lines.

Meals at the lighthouse were molded by the shortage of cash, the lack of
refrigeration, and the abundance of fish. Fresh fish in the summer
and salted in the winter were the dietary mainstays of the family.
Fishing was important for kids and adults. Interestingly, no one
fished much when they arrived in Mackinaw City. It no longer was
financially necessary and apparently was not valued as a recreational
activity.

As you read these stories of the light keeper's children you get the
feeling that dad's job was a family job. Everyone played their part
and for the kids this meant being neat and clean, especially when the
inspector was expected, and being out of sight when the inspector
arrived. Everyone knew that their personal performance might cost
dad his highly valued job. This truly was family work.

John P. Campbell was born August 3, 1898 on Beaver Island or August 3, 1899 at Cross Village. His original birth certificate burned and he was re-issued two birth certificates with two different dates and locations. His parents lived on Beaver Island when Cross Village, including all of the records, burned. When he went to work for the government during the war he had to have a birth certificate. Since none was available he had to get affidavits. Some people said he was born on Beaver Island and some said he was born in Cross Village, so he ended up with two birth certificates. Cross Village is just across the lake and they were back and forth all of the time. He was a Native American and he left home at an early age.

Were your father's parents on Beaver Island? What were they doing?
My grandmother was a cook in lumber camps when they used to do lumbering from Beaver Island and other places. They moved around a lot, through southern Michigan, through Elk Rapids, Cross Village, Harbor Springs, Petoskey, Alba and those areas. My grandfather was a Scotchman, the Campbell name. He was the boss when they set up a camp out in the woods and they cut lumber. That is how he met my grandmother, she was a cook. He married the cook. (Laugh) There were times when they were in the Upper Peninsula also. Those lumber people moved a lot. But he did live in Cross Village for a long, long time.

Where did your grandparents get married?
His name was Archie Campbell. Her name was Myra Fertia. They were married in Bellaire.

When your dad was growing up had your grandfather settled down?
I don't think he ever did settle down. He left, went off on his own. My grand-mother later remarried a couple of times. All I knew was the last husband she had.

What was life like for your dad in Cross Village?
He would have been a young boy when he lived in Cross Village. At an early age, I say real early, I think he was 16 when he enlisted in the army. He really wasn't around Cross Village a whole lot.

Was he in World War I?
Yes, in fact he went to Texas to fight Poncho Villa when the war started. He was in Brownsville, Texas at the time. He was about to go into Mexico when the war started. He was real young because he lied about his age back then. That was common.

Do you have a feeling for why he left?
Not really. Things weren't good then as far as employment. He had worked in the woods a little bit with his dad. That is about all there was back in those days. Plus being an Indian. . . If you are an Indian you are from the other side of the tracks. It was really hard.

So he was labeled as Indian?
Oh, yeah.

Your grandmother has an American sounding name. Was she 100% Indian?
As far as I know. You know how it was with Indians, they took those French names. My father went to Holy Childhood School where they forced Indians to go to school to break them. He went to that in Harbor. It was a pretty tough life back then.

He joined the army, not the navy?
Right. When World War I started he went to the war. He was wounded two different times. Remember the Germans and the story of the gas? He was gassed. The Veterans Administration says that is probably what killed him. He died of lung cancer. It bothered him most of his life.

Did he smoke?
Oh, yes. Smoked and drank. It all went together.

Richard L. Moehl

Dick Campbell talks about his dad

I know the lighthouse service was opposed to drinking. It must not have been opposed to smoking.
Oh, no. Most of the places he was at were so remote that drinking didn't make any difference. It was too hard to carry too much out there to last you very long. As a kid I remember rolling cigarettes for my dad out of the old rollers.

Where was he for the army?
He went overseas in 1917. He was all through France and Germany. He was wounded twice, gun shot wounds to the leg and to the shoulder.

Did it make him limp or anything?
Nope, but he did get a pension for it. Not very much. He did get something. There is a story about that too. This is jumping way ahead. In the depression days, later, when things were really bad, they handed out welfare and all that sort of thing. Working on a lighthouse didn't pay very much. During the winter we couldn't be with my father. There were six of us kids. He was excluded from any handouts because anyone who drew a pension of any kind was not eligible. He got $6.50 a month. Well, back then it was quite a bit but not enough for six kids. So here my father is on starvation wages from the lighthouse and we couldn't get welfare and there were six kids. So if it weren't for the neighbors that were getting welfare, we would never have made it. I can remember my mother sitting at the kitchen table many times crying, wondering where the next groceries were going to come from. If it wasn't for the neighbors. . . Everyone around was getting it. We couldn't get it.

So he came back from the army and he got hooked up with your mother and with the lighthouse service.
He came back to Harbor Springs in late 1919. He worked around there. He worked as a commercial fisherman, taxi driver, worked in the woods. That's when he had the opportunity to work for the government. Even back then they had a preference for wounded veterans. So that is how he got the government job. At that time everybody was in bad shape, it was a good job.

He met your mother in Harbor Springs?
They were in school together previously. My mother was married to a solider who died from influenza. She and my dad were friends from high school. They married in 1920.

How in Harbor Springs would you hear that there was a job with the lighthouse service?
I don't know. Probably something through the veterans. Also there was a light-house there at Harbor Point. I know he was always connected with the veteran's

organizations all his life, so maybe it was through that. That was Federal Civil Service then. That is how the veterans got that preference of 10 points or something. He had at least three kids before he took the test.

Grassy Island - North
1932-1936

What year did he go down and take the test?
He took the test in '29. He took one in October '29 which put him on a preference list. He obtained a score of 88.1 and 70% was the requirement to go on. He did pretty good on that. He took another one in '31. He took the test in March and got the results in July. See, the government was quicker then. In July '31 he obtained the standard for the position of assistant lighthouse keeper. In a letter dated April '32, "You have been appointed subject to taking the oath of office of keeper at the salary of $1,200." He went to Grassy Island in '32.

When we lived on Grassy Island I remember going to my first year of school in the winter. That was a year-round station. My dad used to put us in a boat. It had runners on it. If there was ice on the river he would push us across. Or, if it was open water, we would row. I can remember going to my first or second year of school in Wyandotte. That's where we had to go to school, in Wyandotte. Even though I was very, very young and small I can remember it just like it was yesterday. That was pretty treacherous. But the river there isn't very wide. The island was right out in the middle. Canadians here and Wyandotte on the other side. It didn't take us long to get across, but it wasn't very nice to have to go back and forth to school.

Campbell family photo

The boat with runners used to carry Dick and his sisters to school

He took you every day?
Yes.

Did he get paid every month? Was it seasonal?
No, we were on Grassy Island year round. Almost $110 a month. (Laugh)
And it was a job. I can remember him talking about that, how lucky he was to even
get the job. It was during the depression. He took the first test in October '29, the
depression. He mentioned that several times.

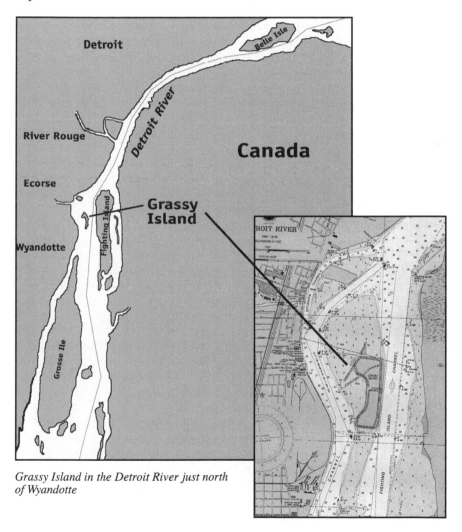

*Grassy Island in the Detroit River just north
of Wyandotte*

Tell us about Grassy Island.

It was just off Wyandotte. It was just a long narrow island, probably 1/4 mile long. It had a lighthouse. On one end they had a range light. They had to take care of aids to navigation up and down the river. They went down as far as Grosse Ile. They used to put the gas tanks in the buoys. Make sure they were lit. We lived there with the keeper. I don't remember if he had any children or not. It was one building, very low wooden structure. Later in the dredging operations Grassy Island disappeared. I talked, over the years, to many of the old time sailors who sailed the lakes. Some of them remember it, the older ones. There is a Grassy Island now. Where it is, I don't know. There is one in Wisconsin but there is one in the Detroit River too. The current Grassy Island is not the one. They dredged it right out of there. It didn't amount to much. It was very narrow, couple of hundred feet wide and real long, made up from fill from some of the plants, factories there for years and years.

The lighthouse was a low wooden structure?
Yes, we have a picture of it here. It was a very nice lighthouse.

Nancy – Your mother didn't like it.
It was so close to things, but you couldn't get to them.

Dick's mother's first glimpse of North Grassy Island

This was her first lighthouse experience?
Yes.

Why do you think it was a good one?
I was so young. It was very interesting, ships passed there constantly. It was in the prohibition days. Down on the end of the island those fast boats used to drop stuff off from the Canadian side. The keepers were supposed to be watching that – part of their duties. Report it. Nothing they could do. No radios, no telephones. There was nothing you could do anyway, so they just ignored it. I can remember that.

They didn't have a radio contact?
Oh, no. Nothing.

When was Grassy Island dredged away?
I don't know. I sailed on the lakes somewhat too and I talked to a lot of old captains. One of them was Cap Shepler. He was in Wyandotte. He lived right up the street from us. In his obituary it doesn't mention it, but he sailed on the cement boats out of Wyandotte, Wyandotte Chemical. They were the little gray boats. I think some of them now belong to LaFarge Cement, over in Alpena. He sailed on those boats.

Dick in the boat on the Detroit River. Dick was born in 1930 so lived on Grassy Island from age two to six.

Let's go back to the Grassy Island house. Was it new when your dad moved there?
I don't think so. I think there were people there ahead of us.

What else do you remember there?
Most of the time riding up and down the river. Us kids could ride on the boat with
them. It wasn't like today with this liability thing. I would go with my father and
the other man, the keeper, and we would go up and down the river. Somewhere
there is a picture of the boat and these gas tanks. It would go along side the buoys.
I was with my dad always. I was real small.

Did they pump gas into these buoys or change out tanks?
No, they were like gas tanks. They were acetylene. They made sure the buoys
were lit.

They must have been pretty heavy tanks.
They were big tanks like the big oxygen tanks of today. Heavy, heavy, miserable
things. My Dad had a quick temper. My son inherited it. You are on this little
wooden boat, taking these tanks out and then you have to crawl up on the top of the
buoy. There was a ring around the top where you could stand, lean back and work
on something. My dad used to get up there with the wrenches, a standard wrench
that was made to fit all these things. His temper was so bad he would get up there
and the wrench would slip off. He'd
bang up his knuckle. Then he would
throw the wrench and, along with it, all
these famous curse words. Well, it got
so that the keeper got a piece of line and
tied it on the wrench and hooked it to
his arm. "So there, now throw your
wrench." That was a big joke always.

They had to account for those.
Oh, did they ever!

Did he dive for it?
Not out there you didn't. It was pretty
wild on the river. Heavy current and
ships. The buoy was usually laying over
unless a ship went by. Then it was

Campbell family photo

*The lighthouse boat equipped for
carrying acetylene tanks on the back
deck*

Jane, Dick, and Helen Campbell at Grassy Island Lighthouse

Campbell family photo

Sandy Planisek

A small two-pocket buoy

bouncing all over and the boat along side. There were a lot of bad things that took place. It isn't like today where everything is so modern.

They actually reached over from in this wooden boat into the buoy and pulled the tank up?
There is a great big plate on the side. You have to take the bolts off and take that plate off. Take the old tanks out. Slip the new ones in.

Was there more than one tank in each one?
Oh yeah, there were quite a few. Of course after you got them all in and turned it on, you had to go up on the top and open the lens and light it.

With just a keeper and assistant at this station, they had to take care of all of these buoys as well as the lighthouse? How was their work day set up that they had time to do all of this and take care of the light?
Once the ice moved in there was very little navigation back then on the Detroit River. That part of it was pretty well shut down. The ice was moving constantly up and down the river. The work day didn't amount to a whole lot except taking care of the lens.

Did they keep the light lit 12 months out of the year?
You know, I don't remember. They probably did. Otherwise we wouldn't have been there. That was before radiobeacons and things like that. We used to get terrible ice in the river.

What do you remember your dad doing around the house?
Like all lighthouses it was paint, paint and paint. Then, of course, they had a little bit of grass they cut. The boat was a big problem because back then it was a wooden boat. We had the skiff and the power boat. That was an open boat for servicing the buoys. There were a lot of things to do. The dock was always coming apart because of the current and ice in the river.

How big were these boats?
The power one we would run up the river with was only about 25 feet at the most. Maybe smaller. The skiff, more like a scow with runners on the bottom, was probably 16 feet. People years ago used them all the time. If the ice was on it you could get the boat up on the ice and slide it on the little runners on the bottom.

The three of you kids went to school that way?
Yes.

What was the school like?
In Wyandotte it was real nice. It was a brand new school.

Where?
It couldn't be too far away. It was very nice.

Scrub brush & all.

John Campbell is scrubbing one of the buildings on Grassy Island

Campbell family photo

Were you treated differently because you were a lighthouse kid?
No, I don't think so.

I see there was an oil house?
(Laugh) They all had oil houses. That oil house was cleaner than most people's houses, painted and otherwise. Everything in its place. Every one was the same.

What was the fuel used by the light in the house?
I don't recall. I know we had a lot of lanterns around there. I can't remember what the lanterns were for. In fact, one picture of my mother shows her standing there with a lantern. But I can't remember what those were used for. Maybe we had kerosene lights in the house.

Was this house like a duplex?
Yes.

Was there any place for a garden?
Not that I recall. There may have been, but I was small.

What do you remember about the lantern room? The lens?
Not too much.

Were you allowed up there?
I don't think I had any occasion to get involved with that at all. I was probably there, but I don't recall it. I was pretty young then.

Did your dad wear his uniform?
Usually only when we knew someone was coming around. They came around quite often there because the depot was right there in Detroit. Back

Edna Campbell in front of the replacement light holding two kerosene lanterns

Campbell family photo

then, when anybody of any authority was to come along to inspect, they flew the inspector's flag on the boat. You could see the tender coming with that inspector's flag. It was large. You knew that they were probably going to stop and look. That was usually the sign. I can't remember back at Grassy Island how they passed the word, somehow the keepers always seemed to know they were coming.

If you were stationed there 12 months did your dad get anything like a vacation?
They did, but I don't know how that worked. Occasionally we used to visit back to Harbor Springs.

Was there another keeper?
Sometimes he was there alone. Just us.

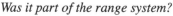

John Campbell in his Lighthouse Service uniform

Stories I hear they had to be up all night watching the light. Do you remember that?
There I don't recall them standing too much of a watch at night. I suppose they had some way to make sure during the night it was lit. I don't recall them sitting there, standing watch.

Was it part of the range system?
On the far end of this little hill was one of those range lights, like Cheboygan has, a tower. The light was on one end and the range on the other so when the ships would make their turn they would line that up.

Campbell family photo

Dick watching as the Campbell family arrived at the dock on Grassy Island

Was your light the front range light?
Yeah. Because on the far end, on the fill, way out in the swamp area, I forget what they called it, a semaphore or something. They had a name for that out there. It was painted red or orange and had a red light on it.

What color was this light?
I don't know. It wasn't real large. Of course Cheboygan isn't real large either (Cheboygan River Front Range Light). My dad knew quite a bit about Cheboygan when he first came to Mackinaw. He knew Clarence Land real well. He used to go down there a lot. It bounced back and forth then with the Coast Guard and the lighthouse.

Why did your dad leave Grassy Island?
He wanted to get out of the city and out of that area. The word would get out that so-and-so was going to quit or retire. There would be an opening. You could apply for this. I guess what you did was just write a letter asking to go there. Whether they made an official advertisement back then, I don't know. I know he did write several times for different lights. He really didn't care where he was, except he wanted out of there, because of the remoteness and so forth. Well, there was no life whatsoever.

The keeper wasn't old enough to be retiring?
No

The Campbell family moved to Wyandotte when the manned lighthouse was replaced with an automated tower. One of the family photos says that North Grassy Island was the last oil light on the Great Lakes.

John and Dick on the new base

Campbell family photos

Dick eating watermelon at the new tower

Ron Benjamin of Hesperia, MI sent us the following (Sept, 1990):

"My stepfather, John (Jack) Campbell entered the lighthouse service in either 1929 or 1930. His first assignment was Grassy Island in the Detroit River. The residence contained the front range light for vessels heading south, a nightly boat patrol was made north to the mouth of the Rouge River and south to Grosse Ile. The dwelling was later replaced and the living quarters moved to Van Alstyne Blvd. in Wyandotte, where motor patrols augmented the boat patrols.

"Dad's other assignments included Huron Island in Lake Superior, Old Mackinac Point in Mackinaw City and Point Betsie Light at Frankfort on Lake Michigan. During the fall of 1936 I worked on the Gray's Reef Lighthouse in upper Lake Michigan. We lived in wooden frame quarters sitting on the lighthouse apron and fastened to the light with cables."

The lighthouse being torn down and replaced by an automated tower

Huron Island
1936-1944

He applied to several and then what?
There was an opening at Huron Island, so he accepted that. In the meantime, he spent some time in Harbor Springs, where my other grandmother lived, Grandma Wright. We spent some time there and he went smelt fishing one time at Sturgeon Bay. In the process they were pushing a car up the road on a hill. I know right where it is, a sandy old hill. The bumpers got caught and he got out to jump on the bumper to break it loose. He broke it loose. His own car rolled back over him, right across his chest and smashed all of his ribs. So he couldn't take his position on Huron Island on time. Here he was laying in bed all taped up with tire tracks across him. He couldn't get there on time and he was afraid he was going to lose the job. This is why I remembered it.

Why go to Huron Island, that turned into a seasonal job?
It was seasonal, yes, but you also know that in winter, for a while, you were off the island. You did what you wanted to do. Well then, when the war started, the government got real nasty about it. They said, "Why those guys aren't doing

anything. We've got to find a job for them." So a couple of years he had to go to Detroit and spend the winter at the depot fixing buoys, whatever, boats, things like that. Then, as the war progressed, he spent a couple of winters on the ice patrol. They had it up on the north end. It was to watch commercial fishermen, search and rescue. They sent him over to Jacobsville. He was at Jacobsville at the light. They sent a whole bunch of guys. They didn't have anything for them to do. But they wanted them to work. Then he spent some time at Portage Entry. He taught recruits then. My father, having previous military service, was a real candidate for training recruits. He didn't like any part of it because he was used to being home all winter. They paid him during the winter even though it was seasonal. These were some of the duties he had to do at different times.

When he started was he working for the lighthouse service?
Yes. There was a date when they got letters saying you could, more or less insinuating that you had better, transfer into the Coast Guard. I suppose for security reasons. They would give you a rank equal to your civil service. That is how he ended up what he was. He was a bosun first class in the Coast Guard. They forced him to do it because of his age and previous military service. Well since then, over the years, I have heard that they didn't force them. He could have stayed as a civilian. But, they didn't guarantee them their jobs if they stayed because of security reasons. His big problem was because of his previous military service and as young as he was, he was going to end up back in the war again. Luckily, he didn't. He stayed here training recruits up at Portage Entry and things like that. At that time we lived in Baraga. We lived in the reservation. You know where the "rez" is up there? You know where the casino is?

At Sand Hill, at Ahmeek, up Portage Entry there was a barracks there. Did he train there?
That's the one. At Portage Entry. Sand Hills. Behind the Sand Hills Light there was a brick building. This was a barracks for military people. I remember going there. But Portage Entry light was right there too.

He did that in the winter and came back to Huron Island in the summer?
Right.

What do you remember about Huron Island?
I went there when I was pretty young. It was really nice. This all goes back to why I am like I am. I learned to be alone. I loved it. You had to survive on your own ideas. Your ideas, whatever you did. To this day I am still that way.

Who else was there when you got there?
Jim Collins was keeper. My dad was first assistant. Martin Peterson, an old Norwegian, was second assistant. Great old guy.

Did they have kids?
Martin didn't, but Jim Collins did. He had four or five. Some of them still live in L'Anse and Baraga. They are involved with the Huron Island preservation.

Was Martin a bachelor?
No, he had a wife but no children. Much older.

What was it like for you?
It was great with all us kids. Collins kids, three or four of those our age. We spent our summers out there. When school started we had to get off.

You weren't there as much as your dad? He came earlier and stayed later?
Yes.

John Campbell
maude P.
Jim Collins
Laura Collins
Huron Isl.
1943
" Clean up crew

Campbell family photo

1942

"See that funny looking hat? Dad would take an old felt hat and cut just the crown out of it. Remember Skeeziks? Remember the hat, the skull hat? He would take a pair of scissors and make designs. Actually, it was to keep the dirt out of his hair and to keep his hair from blowing around. He always had some pin stuck on it."

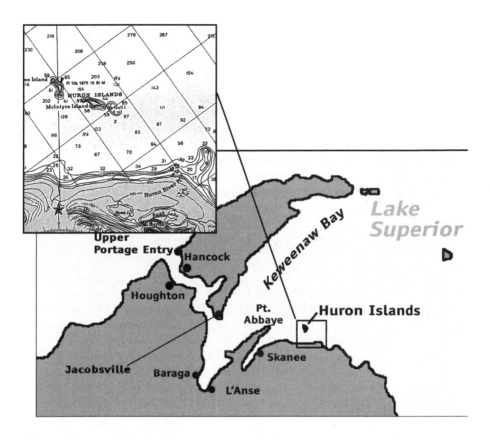

Where did you go to school?
Went to school some in L'Anse and some in Baraga. That is when we lived on the
"rez" in Baraga.

You stayed up there? You didn't come back to Harbor Springs?
The last couple of years we came back and we lived in Pellston. We had a house in
Pellston at one time. We spent our time between Pellston, L'Anse, and Baraga. I
went to school there.

Where would you take off from for Huron Island?
Skanee. I've seen different things about how far it was. Some people say a few
miles, some people say more. I always figured it was about 14 miles. It is a few
miles directly to shore, to the Huron Mt. Range. The rock outcropping runs all the
way from Skanee to Big Bay and Marquette. We were only like five miles from
the shore, but there was nothing there but mountains. It was 14 miles from Skanee.

And Skanee was a little place like Van or Levering. There was one building that contained a post office, gas station, and grocery. We used to dock at a commercial fishermen's dock. They used to let us come in there.

What kind of a boat?
There was a 26-foot open boat when we went there. It was a real nice wooden boat with hoops on the front you could pull back for splash. It wasn't very big. These Finnish people up around Chassell built these. Later they built us another wooden boat. It was probably about 20 feet long. It had a cabin on it with a gasoline engine in it. That was pretty nice. But it was pretty wild going back and forth. You know Lake Superior, it's different.

Did it have a name?
No, can't have names. The government boats didn't have names.

That is the boat you took to Skanee?
Yes, when we got back to the island it always had to be pulled out of the water. You never left it at the dock because of the weather. The dock was way at the other end of the island so you couldn't keep an eye on it. There was a winch in the boat house. It was a cement boat house.

Huron Island looking north

A hand-operated winch?
Yep, and one person could crank that boat up. Underneath, in the water, is a cradle so when you got everything ready you pulled the boat onto the cradle, hooked the line on the bow, and pulled it up into the boathouse. You had to do that because it wasn't safe to leave a boat in the water at any time.

The weather there is tremendous. In one hour's time it might be coming right over the top of that dock. And once it starts, there is no saving the boat. Nothing you can do with two or three men out there. The only time the boat was in the water was when we went ashore. It was a gasoline Kermath engine. It was brand new, but back then there were always problems, gas engines and boats.

How did your food supplies come?
We had to go ashore and buy it. We had no refrigeration when we first went to Huron Island. No refrigeration, no running water. All water had to be carried from the lake. You never went to the lake, to the boat house or the fog signal unless you took a couple of pails with you. Even us kids, we carried back water.

The boat being lowered from the boat house

Campbell family photo

You went into L'Anse to buy your groceries. You didn't boat all the way around did you?
No, there was Pt. Abbey. Skanee is on one side. We went straight along the shore into Skanee. Then it is six or eight miles by road to L'Anse. It was pretty crude back then. The roads were pretty terrible. But in Skanee there was just a post office and small grocery store combined. That's all there was there. There was an A&P store in L'Anse. It was pretty good size. Ford Motor company had a mill there. Ford owned a whole lot of property there. He got the lumber to make those old woodies. It was a big mill. Later some paper company bought it. Ford had a fleet of tugs and barges that he hauled that wood down to the Detroit area. The mill was great.

What were your chores?
You are talking about a chore to get the water. It was a real chore.

There was a lot of roaming. Not too much in the cleaning part of it. There was not too much to clean outside because the wind blew most of the dirt away. But water was the big thing. You never went down or back without carrying one pail or two pails. For us kids they would take gallon paint cans, when the paint was used, clean them all out and put a bail on them. There was always a bunch of them sitting there. So if you went to the lake, you always came back with water. You better not come back without water. You can imagine kids carrying two cans of water slopping it around, falling down, whatever. By the time you got up to the house it was probably dirty and warm. But that

John Campbell, Jim Collins, Stanley McBride - Huron Island - 1936

Campbell family photo

Carrying water in pails

was one of the main things. We had the old farm bucket with a dipper to drink. The water sat there with a dipper in it. You had to be careful. You might get up in the middle of the night thirsty and if no one had carried any water you might go back to bed thirsty.

We had to carry all our groceries up there. When you went ashore once a week or every 10 days everyone had to pack everything up to the house. Most of the time you spent the rest of the day or night hauling it up because you didn't want to leave it down at the boat house. Perishables, no such things. Maybe for a day or so. There was no refrigeration. Bread would mold. My mother would bake bread. But we ate lots of fish and boiled potatoes. It would keep.

It doesn't look like Huron Island had a garden.
No. No, there was no garden.

What would be served for meals?
Weather permitting, the boat went ashore every 10 days or so. The first few days we might have a lot of things. As it grew closer to the end and the weather was bad, food got pretty scarce. The one thing we had a lot of was fish. We did a lot of fishing.

The kids?
Oh, yeah.

And the adults?
Oh, yeah. Because my father and the other guys used to catch fish. The commercial fishermen would stop by, they fished that area too, and they would pick up our fish and take them to L'Anse and sell them to the A&P store where we bought most of our groceries. They would take our fish in and sell them and we would get credit towards our groceries. We did a lot of that. And, of course, we ate lots of fish. We smoked lots of fish.

Did your folks get an allowance for food?
No. No allowance for food.

What was the pay there?
I don't know. This grocery thing was very interesting. Only one person went ashore at a time unless somebody was going in to a doctor and had to stay, or on vacation. In the summer, when I was there, I went with the boat every time whoever went.

What did you have for breakfast?
We couldn't have milk because of no refrigeration. We would go to the A&P; they sold evaporated milk. We would buy cases and cases of it. But you don't use it directly out of the can. You had to dilute it. Everybody had a different idea what the mix was. Today I couldn't stand the taste of it, but back then it was good. The best way to drink evaporated milk, when it is diluted, is ice cold. But no refrigeration. You would get up in the morning, you might have corn flakes or oatmeal with this evaporated milk. It was fine, that was all that there was. You got used to it. That was it. I drank cases of it. We all did.

Did you have Eagle Brand?
Oh yeah, Eagle Brand. Once in a while my mother made something out of Eagle Brand. But I can't remember what it was. It was real thick. Later years, the last year or so we were there, the Coast Guard came up with an oil-fired refrigerator. It had a wick in there, a tank on the bottom. It smoked up your house terrible. You had to clean the wick everyday and fill the tank. Well, they worked real well. This was the early days of that type of refrigeration. So when we got that we could hold a few things for a while as long as it worked. But it was very unreliable.

My mother bought Eagle Brand and somehow she mixed it and we made ice cream in there. It had a little freezer in the top when it worked. It was very unreliable. When it worked us kids were just wild about that ice cream made in those ice cube trays. We thought it was great. Maybe it wasn't. It was creamy.

Was the lake used for cooling stuff?
It was too far away.

Was there any thought of an ice house?
No, there was nobody out there to cut ice. You couldn't put it anywhere anyway.

That was breakfast, how about lunch?
One thing we had was lots of potatoes. We had fish and boiled potatoes. Boiled fish, boiled potatoes. Sometimes boiled together. I learned real quick from Martin Peterson. He was an old Norwegian, they made what you call fish bouillabaisse. Well, it is actually boiled fish and onions and carrots and everything put together like a stew almost. It was delicious. To this day I can eat it every day. It's really good. Throw the potatoes in. So we had a lot of fish and a lot of potatoes. That was toward the end of the grocery line. Here is what my dad used to do. I tell this story because I know people don't believe it and they probably gag when they

listen. I went out there after school started one time. I had broken my arm and they said I couldn't go to school. "You go for a couple of weeks and be with your father on the lighthouse." This was in November, when the storms were bad. So I went out there. You couldn't keep bread because it would mold or dry out and not be any good. It would be a week or two weeks before you would get ashore. So he used to take and make pancakes, all kinds of them. Fire up the stove and make a big kettle. He would only make them a certain size, about that big around (4 inches). He put them in those Mother's Oat boxes, those round ones. He would stack them in there. He would make three or four boxes. In November it is cold and you could set them outside. You didn't need any refrigeration. That was our bread. If you made a sandwich, that was your bread. You know what happens to pancakes after they sit a while like that, they get all soggy and slippery. Some people think, oh my god, how could you eat them? But they were good.

What did you put between these?
It could be anything, maybe nothing, maybe some syrup, jelly, anything. That was the way they all did it. It worked. They got pretty stale by the time dad got to the end. When he would make them, he would make sure they would fit in there. He would stack them with nothing in between them.

Were there animals on the island?
We had a lot of rabbits, but we didn't eat the rabbits. They had some kind of disease or something. Different times we would kill them and when you pulled the hide off there would be blisters in there. We would never eat them.

How did your mother feel about going out there? She got to spend two-thirds of the year in town with conveniences and electricity. Did she look forward to going there for the summer?
Oh, yes, she did. There was no school. We could run and do what we wanted. There was so much that we all missed. Everything. Like my wife says, that is why you don't go anywhere and do anything today. You just never grew up with it. And I didn't. I got to the point where I didn't care and don't care.

It looks like there are two houses.
Yes. Originally before we went there, everybody lived in the big stone lighthouse. That was a 2-family thing, upstairs and down. But you shared the kitchen. That little lean-to on the back was the kitchen. Originally everyone was just in the stone house.

Lighthouse   Wooden house

Privy

Michigan State Archives

A recent aerial of the light station. The lighthouse did not have dormers when the Campbells lived on Huron Island

But in later years, just before we went there, they built that white frame building. That was where we lived. Martin and his wife, Maude, lived in the back of it. We both had kitchens there. Everybody cooked for themselves.

So the stone lighthouse was the keeper's quarters?
Yes. When all the kids and wives left in the fall, usually the three men would get together and share the meals. But they stood watches too, so sometimes there would only be two there, or one at the house.

Did the two men move back into the stone house?
No, they stayed in their houses.

What about the privy?
That privy dated back as far as the lighthouse. Like most lighthouses, they are brick with copper roofs. It was a three holer and it even had one for little kids. It was painted up in there beautiful and kept just as clean. On the back side it dropped right off, straight down into the lake. Once a year, late in the fall, they had a big wooden box on the back side, they would open that door and give it a push and it went right on over into the lake. That is how they emptied it. All the walkways there were planked. You had to because it was so uneven. The walk was three 2 by 12s wide with cleats nailed on it so you wouldn't slip and fall. The privy was down quite an angle. From the outhouse it dropped off to nothing. When I was

young, for some reason, I had a terrible habit of walking in my sleep. My mother would just about go crazy. One time I got up in the middle of the night and walked down right past the privy and off the edge. There was a bunch of garbage and stuff that I landed in. There I was naked, and I fell off there. By that time my mother was wondering where I was. Several times I walked in my sleep. My mother didn't know what to do. Tie a rope on me. This was a close call.

Our outhouse had a trough around the roof. Let me tell you how close they were with their money. They couldn't get any gutter to put around it on their budget. So my dad and Jim Collins started saving tin cans. They all had to be the same size. Back then they made tin cans heavy. They were real tin cans. They would take the top and bottom out, slit them, and solder them together. They did that all the way around. The idea was to use the water to flush it out, but it didn't work. They really didn't need it because they had that big box that they slid over the side every year.

We lived in the front part of the wooden house, back as far as the double window. On the back was a kitchen and a bedroom where Martin Peterson lived back there. They lived in the back.

United States Coast Guard

The privy is the small building on the right

Did the furniture belong to the government or your family?
Most of it was homemade stuff. The rest of it was, we might have taken some there, but it was pretty crude. We had some homemade beds, my dad would make the frame. They would buy a mattress and springs. We had some chairs. But when the Coast Guard came, they used to drag in a lot of stuff. The Coast Guard had all kinds of stuff. They brought some bunk beds and chairs and tables. The basics. Like you would have in a boot camp or something. Before they got there it was mostly handmade stuff.

In later years we ended up with bunk beds. I think the government sent those up there. Previous to that we just had homemade beds. I didn't share a bed. Times were hard. I remember my father would go down in the woods there and cut down some balsam or fir and make the bed for the bottom. Instead of having springs he could get screen. They had lots of rolls of screen. He tacked screen all the way around. If we had a mattress or a whole bunch of blankets to lay on top of there that was our bed. Of course it sagged. They were nice. We really liked them.

The house we lived in had a nice floor. All the floors were nice except the lighthouse had 40 coats of paint on it, gray paint. They didn't varnish the floors, not at any lighthouse until we got here (Old Mackinac Point). The wainscoting on Huron Island was all painted.

The plank walkway was elevated. There were places that it was touching the ground and other places where it might be six or eight feet over the rocks. So you wouldn't slip on it when it rained they nailed cleats about every foot.

Did you have to clean the wood?
No, but it was slippery.

There were five kids?
Yes.

The wooden house looks like about 12 by 15 feet.
Yes, we had bunk beds. We didn't have a living room or anything. It was all one big room. It was big to me. The kitchen was back by the window.

You had a kitchen and they had a kitchen?
Yes, but the kitchen didn't amount to much because we didn't have running water. All we had was an old kerosene stove with the wicks in it. It smoked all the time and smelled up the house. That was what you cooked on. Later years we had a refrigerator that had a wick in it. It isn't like a kitchen today. Some small cupboards. The table was right by this window.

What did you do about bathing?
In the lake. This brings up another story. The water we carried by buckets from the lake was the only drinking water. What would we do about bathing? We went to the lake. What about washing dishes? There was very little water. There were times, not always, when you sat and ate off your plate. Then the next meal you would turn it over and eat off the other side. This was just when the men were there, eat on the back side, because water was scarce. That's a true story. Not when my mother was there but usually when just the keepers were there, or I was with them, when there wasn't anybody around. You know how you put things in the sink, use water to wash the dishes? We didn't have a sink, just a wash basin.

Wooden house layout

What kind of plates were they that you could eat on the back?
We didn't have any good stuff out there. Everything was transported back and forth, it broke. In later years, the Coast Guard came up with some old stuff they had.

They were ceramic plates?
Yes, you know there is a little ridge around there. That worked pretty good to hold it. You talk to my sister she would say, "He is crazy, that never happened." But she wasn't there when this was happening. I was.

What about washing clothes?
The other source of water was a cistern, but it was terrible. There was a name for the kitchen that was added on to the lighthouses over the years, the lean-to. Right under there they had a cistern. Out there it was solid rock. It was a pretty big cistern. How they worked to dig it, I don't know. It was under the kitchen floor. All the drain troughs, it was copper with a slate roof, beautiful and would last forever, ran into that. They weren't too careful about it. There were birds, mice, and just anything in it. So you couldn't drink it. In the lighthouse itself there was a pitcher pump and a sink and a pipe that ran out to get rid of the water. If you were real careful, and not after a rain which would rile up the cistern, the water was pretty good. Sometimes it did smell. My mother used all kinds of things, like bleach, to cover it. That is where most of the wash water for clothes came from, out of the cistern. You wouldn't dare drink it. It was contaminated definitely.

This recent photo shows the original fog signal building and the modern barracks added by the Coast Guard (white building).

How often did you bathe and have your clothes washed?
Not as often as you would think. We were down by the lake most of the time, if we weren't swimming we were splashing around in the boat. My mother washed clothes a lot.

Was the water cold?
Ohhh, clear as a bell. Very cold.

What about the adults?
My dad used to go in the water a lot. He'd go splashing around in there. But there was no beach. It was all rock. The only thing you could do was find a nice place on the rock. Jump in and you usually came out pretty fast too.

Did they teach you to swim?
Just us kids learned together, I guess. My mother, I can just imagine what she thought. We would take off in the morning and she wouldn't see us for the rest of the day. On this island, we were either out in the rowboat or swimming. She would look out and we might be way out. I can just see her pulling her hair out.

How many times did you get hurt?
None. Good thing.

Tell us about the picture of the three of you sitting on a bench. Was the kitchen in the door of the lean-to I see? I see a chimney vent there.
No, there was no vent off the kitchen stove. That is why the ceilings were all brown and your clothes smelled like it. You had to clean the wick all the time. You got kind of lazy about cleaning the wick. But upstairs that was all one room. Later years, when the Coast Guard took it over, they put dormers in and divided it into rooms.

How about the guitar. Was music a part of your life out there?
No, my older sister, Helen, she always wanted a guitar. They bought her one for Christmas one year. She never did learn to play it. That is it.

Maude Peterson had no children. She just loved kids. She probably bought us these hats. I don't remember wearing a straw hat very much. Maude just liked us kids. She was always doing something for us.

Campbell family photo

The kids, Dick, Diana Dawn, Kathleen, sitting in the "meeting place" on the rock behind the lean-to kitchen. The kitchen was in the left side and the battery bank was in the right side, through the door.

Tell us something about your shoes.
It looks like old high tops. Usually we went bare foot. Apparently these were left over from winter. We had a pair of tennis shoes for the summer and in the winter I went to those old high tops. That was two pairs of shoes a year. Normally we ran around with bare feet.

Were the tennis shoes for when the inspector came?
Usually they made us get out of sight. Go where you usually go when we can't find you. Occasionally we would get down by the boat when they were coming or leaving. The crew members would talk to us. They would give us little things they might have in their pockets. We liked that because we didn't get to talk to people. Those crew members were really nice. To get there they had to come on the tender. The tender would anchor off half a mile or so. They would lower their motor boat and a little barge. Whatever they were bringing to us they would lower onto the barge and come ashore to where that tramway was. When the big shots were gone looking at the other things, us kids would get to talk to the other guys. One time,

Campbell family photo

Moving supplies up to the lighthouse area on top of the island

I remember, I got to go out to the tender while they were hauling. I think his name was Captain Berg. It was on the *Marigold*. I got to eat dinner with him. Captain Berg, he took me in and I ate dinner. That was a big thing, a real big thing.

What are these guys pulling here?
What they are doing there is pulling a fuel tank. Perhaps they had to get down in that gorge. It was quite deep in there. It was always wet in there and tiger lilies grew in there. It was probably eight feet down. You can see that this is Coast Guard doing this. See the hats. That one guy has a seaman's hat. When they came up that trail, all the way from the boat house, the tank couldn't have been in that position. The trail is not that wide. There was an iron pipe railing. But when they got to the ravine, they had to come across the bridge. After they got here they were almost to the oil house.

What came up the tram?
Anything used at the fog signal.

They unloaded at two spots?
Yes, mostly at the boat house. Very little at the signal because it wasn't as good a spot.

Michigan State Archives

The fog signal is in the foreground with the newer barracks building in back. The tender arrived from the right side of the photo and the tram ran down the gentler slope on that side.

How high is the fog signal?
It isn't very high. Solid rock. Probably 50 feet down to the water.

This is where the tram came up?
The tram came up the west side on the gradual slope. On the other side is a big gorge. You could run a boat up in there.

Why did they put the fog signal out here?
Point Abbey is over this way. Most of the shipping that went through here went through the canal at Houghton and Hancock. Nowadays most of the shipping goes out to the end of the Keweenaw Peninsula. The boats are too big and it's a lot easier.

So not many boats got close to this?
Not many. In bad weather we used to get a lot of them by there because they didn't want to go out around the end of the point. They had good shelter, plus they could cut off time going through the canal or just sit in there while the weather was bad.

It would seem that you would want the fog signal where the light was, unless it was just a matter of moving supplies.

I'm sure that was the reason. For heat we had a coal stove to keep warm. They would have to bring the coal on a little barge from the tender in canvas bags. The crew members had to carry them on their back like pack sacks. The lighthouse keepers didn't do that. It was the crew from the tender that did that. Same way with fuel oil or gasoline. It came in 50-gallon barrels. They put it on that little tramway. They put four or five barrels on there, hoist it up, then they would have to empty those barrels. They'd take them back with them. Sometimes they would leave them and exchange them.

That was all crew work, not lighthouse work?

They would take the old empty barrels that were there and leave full ones. Emptying the full barrels was one of the jobs I used to get in on to help my dad. It was really somewhat dangerous because we were dealing with gasoline. We would put an air hose on the 50-gallon barrel and blow the gas out into the big tanks. That is how it was done. Otherwise it would take forever to empty a 50-gallon barrel.

While we were there a couple of years, in the summer, the Corps of Engineers came with their big barges and cranes. They took boulders off the side of the island and took them to Marquette and put them in the breakwater. The boulders came off the side of this island. They were great big ones. They were beautiful rocks.

Your dad spent eight hours of every 24 down at the fog signal. What else were his duties?

That was a pretty big building. A lot of machinery in there. That's where the tramway was. Every lighthouse had to have a tramway. I forget who the guy was in the early days of the lighthouse who came up with these tramways. It was a name they used to curse all the time. He was the guy that started tramways. Everyone had to have a tramway because of so-and-so. It worked good, it really did. It was at a 45 degree angle and they'd have to get all their gasoline, all the fuel oil, everything up it. The tender couldn't dock at the island. They would anchor off and they had a barge with a motorboat that towed it in. The crews would unload all these bags and barrels and boxes. Put it on the tramway and up at the fog signal they had an air operated winch, with all kinds of pulleys and cables, and they would tow it up this 45 degree slope and there was a turntable. Unload everything. All those 50-gallon drums had to be emptied by air and put into a big storage tank. Take them all back down and take them back out to the tender.

You would empty the gasoline out while the tender was waiting?
Sometimes they would wait for the whole thing and sometimes just part of it. It was all done by hand.

It also sounds dangerous.
Very dangerous.

Did the inspectors say or do anything about you selling fish?
No one ever mentioned it. In the fall of the year trout spawn. Late in the fall, when the kids were gone, the spawning of lake trout was just tremendous. I was out there and saw them. My dad, during the summer, would take fish in to the A&P store in L'Anse and trade them for groceries. The butcher used to get lard in wooden kegs that would hold five gallons or less. He would dig the lard out and put it in the showcase. A&P sold lots of it. This butcher, who took care of the A&P, would save these lard kegs for my dad. So every time they might get one or two kegs they would bring them back. When the spawning season came on in the fall they would start fishing and fillet them and salt them in the lard kegs. Then when the tender came to pick them up they would take down their duffle bag and whatever they were taking home with them. There would be 25 or 30 lard kegs of fish. So the tender crew knew what they were doing. They hauled the fish into Houghton and unloaded them. From there my dad would take them home. So all winter long we ate salted lake trout. They never did say anything.

One year our friendly DNR were at the dock and they seized all the fish. I guess they got part of it back because it was illegal, way back then. No license and that many fish. I can remember that. That winter we didn't have as many fish. You always kept the salted fish out in the shed where it was cold. Again, where we lived we didn't have much refrigeration. The first half of the keg was pretty good. You would take out the salted fish, soak them overnight to get the salt off. Delicious, delicious. Time went by and you got down to the bottom of the keg. The salt had kind of treated the fish pretty good. You never did get all of the salt off. The bottom of the keg had pretty salty fish, I tell you. They were delicious. He'd bring in lots of fish in the fall. Of course, the lighthouse crews expected that. Our dads used the small boat and the other boat to do all the fishing. The men themselves didn't have a boat of their own. So we were using government boats for that.

Did you say that some of this was done with gill netting?
Some of it was, but you didn't really have to. The fish were so abundant. In the fall like that, you could throw a hook over the side. When trout are spawning they

are mad and they will bite anything. Beautiful. Nobody ever got out there except a few commercial fishermen that came out from Skanee or maybe L'Anse. The weather was terrible in the fall so it was all our own. We never had to worry about the law or anything.

What did you do when it rained?
I used to spend most of my time down at the signal. They didn't just work their regular watch down there. They had to work other than the watch. We were always doing something down there. That's where I got all of my mechanical ability. How to do it cheap and alone. Do it by hand. Think about it awhile and do with what you have.

Did you have some kind of church service?
No, every day was the same.

How did you communicate with your dad in the spring and the fall?
We used to send letters which had to go to Skanee. It would wait until they picked up the mail every 10 days or so. When the weather got bad, they didn't get ashore. Sometimes it might be a month before they got ashore. We would send it to Skanee to the post office. That was it.

Did you go with him to see him off and pick him up at Skanee?
Sometimes. Some of the guys had a car that they would leave at the dock. My mother would go over there. We docked at a commercial fishermen's dock. You could leave a vehicle. Some of the guys that were single, like the Coast Guardsmen, left their vehicle setting there or if you were rich enough to have a second vehicle. Only in the summer did we leave the car at the dock.

When the Coast Guard got involved they used to send one or two guys. Usually there was only one. The keepers could never figure out what they were supposed to be doing there. These guys stood watches and did work around also. They lived in the big house upstairs. They were young kids enlisted in the Coast Guard. They didn't want to be there, homesick. But nice kids.

Why did they suddenly need more people?
We had some others besides that too. In the civilian days they did it with a lot less. When the Coast Guard came they used a lot of extra people.

Paint.
We used to get a lot of linseed oil, five gallon cans of it. There was a lot of wood and it was a preservative. It was used to cheat a little, to extend the paint if there wasn't enough. They had that figured. Your job was based on how efficient you could run. If last year you got X gallons of paint, you better not order an extra gallon the next year. And it better be painted as good as the previous year.

Did everything get painted every year?
Practically. There were very few things that didn't get painted.

Do you remember them making whitewash?
Yes, but I don't remember the ingredients. Everybody had a different idea about the whitewash. But what I do remember about it was the amount of salt to put in the whitewash. That was crucial. I used to hear them discuss it quite often. The salt had a lot to do with it, especially exterior. The guys knew how to do that. It was as good as paint. Wasn't there something else? Didn't they call it calcimine paint? It was similar to whitewash. It wasn't really supposed to be used in that application. But sometimes someone would come up with that. It worked and it was good. It was water based.

Was that true that you had to turn in an old paint brush to get a new paint brush?
You didn't give it away. They took it. You had to have it. With everything, any tool of any kind. If you break it, you don't throw it away or dispose of it. You had to show it. They disposed of it. Then you would get another one. If you wanted something extra, not replacing, just something extra, then that was an act of Congress. Why do you need that?

I can understand that. Those were depression days. They were trying to run on a budget. But you also had a report card. They kept track of you that way. If you put in for a station and you had a bad reputation, say overspending, that would put you down the list.

These three guys together had to make these decisions. Was that a problem? Did they get along well?
Oh, yeah. They got along real well. Both of them had been in it for so long that they knew the system. They knew if they didn't do it right they weren't going to be there.

How did the day go? What was the routine?
They stood watches. I think they were 8-hour watches, if I remember right. But they stood the watch at the far end of the island at the fog signal. That's a long way away. The light was up on the top. One end was the boat house and that end, about a quarter mile away, was the fog signal. It was just a little trail up through there.

How long would it take to walk down there?
Oh, probably 30 minutes down that trail. Maybe less.

They stood watch at the fog signal in case they had to light it up?
Right. Whoever was off watch was up at the house. Well, originally they had a battery bank with two generators in the lighthouse. They would run the generators and charge the batteries. Over the years the batteries all went haywire. So it got to the point that they had to run a generator at night. As soon as it turned dark they had to start the generator to run the light. During the day we would shut it off. So we would have no electricity in the houses unless you went over and started the generator. Back in those days generators were terrible. They had those old Leroy engines, they called them. They didn't run only half the time. The men were always working on them. They had two of them side-by-side. They were very unreliable. And we had dirty gas. You name it. Yes, gasoline, noisy. Inside the building on the side. They wouldn't replace the batteries all of the years we were there. They wouldn't hold a charge. They had these great big banks of batteries. But down at the other end, at the fog signal, they had a big diesel generator down there. That ran all the time because they had to have lights down there and they had the radiobeacon. In later years they had a radiotelephone.

Was it an electric fog signal?
We had two big diesel engines. They were horizontal with one cylinder and big flywheels on them. We had two of them, if one failed the other would take over. It was air. Great big tanks. They were miserable things – terrible. You started them with a torch. You would heat the head. You had to heat the glow plug. They started on gasoline but they converted it over to diesel. The damn things would run backwards sometimes. Once they got going they would run forever. But to get everything working right you had to be pretty mechanically inclined.

Was one of these keepers always down there?
Yes, but in the early days before radiotelephone they had a big old radio that looked something like a Halicrafter. I don't know what brand it was, but it was a terrible looking thing. In the keeper's dwelling they had a shelf that it was on. Of course this was back in AM days, it was all static. Reception was terrible. Twice a day,

like four in the morning and four in the afternoon, or something like that, out of Marquette they would broadcast messages to all the lights. If it was scratchy and noisy you'd miss it. Sometimes it came clear as a bell. Most of the time no. Everybody had their ear up to it. Anything new that might happen, all official business of course. No foolishness, see. That's when they used to pass the word if the tender was in the area with inspectors. They had little different codes. They didn't say so and so is in the area or anything like that. They had different ways.

What was Marquette, a base?
Yes. Just the radio. Where they used to leave from and go back to in the spring and fall was Houghton. The tender would make the rounds picking everybody up and take them into Houghton. Same way in the spring when they took them. Sometimes they picked them up at Marquette but usually it was Houghton. Everybody would have to be there on a certain day.

Did he spend mostly the daytime down there?
No, they rotated. It wasn't quite as demanding as some stations because the radiobeacon was the most demanding thing. Radiobeacons came about the time we left there. It wasn't too demanding. You just had to watch for fog and the light being on. From the fog signal, which was like a quarter mile away down through the rock, you could see the light. So, occasionally, they could get a lot of sleep on the night shift unless it was bad weather. Back then everybody watched the barometer. If you are a barometer person you can learn a whole lot.

Did they call it the glass?
The glass.

Did you go down there to see him?
I used to be with my dad all the time. We were constantly painting or cleaning all of the time. There was a lot of that. On the boat, rowboats. If I wasn't out on my own or with my sisters playing around doing something, I was with him. I don't know if he liked it or not but I was trailing behind him most of the time. I would think that sometimes he would like it because I would help him with things. At least I thought I was helping him. There were a lot of things I am sure that he appreciated that we did, I did, especially being the boy. Painting, cleaning, carrying things. I'm sure he found a lot of jobs that were probably unnecessary but, anyway, it was really interesting. To this day I credit him for all the little handy things that I think I can do.

Did he eat all his meals with you?
Oh no, it was too far to come back. He would carry a sandwich.

Did your dad try to eat one meal with the family every day?
Yes, sometimes he would get more than that, depending on his watch. The photo that shows us kids sitting up on the rock, that was the focal point you might say of the social life. When you weren't doing anything and the weather was nice we would all sit out there and talk and eat. It's way up on the top of the rock, by the light. You could see for miles up in the mountains or on the shore in the Keweenaw Peninsula. He would spend a lot of time with us. That was really nice in the summer. We spent a lot of time fishing. We had gill nets. We sold the fish. Of course, out there nobody worried about the law because you would see them once a year maybe. It was too far to go.

Somewhere your dad learned a lot of engine repair skills.
If you didn't, you weren't there. You had to make do.

Where did he learn that?
I guess trial and error. You had to be mechanically inclined. That's all there was to it. Otherwise, you would never make it. You had to tackle whatever broke. Either make a part or. . . It would take months, maybe the whole season, to get a part.

This is a skiff or a canoe?
Those are those original lighthouse rowboats. They had a place for two people to row. They were beautiful. One person could row them. They were unbelievable. But when the Coast Guard took over they came through and surveyed everything. They said well, we're going to change this, we are going to get rid of these boats. So they made my dad burn that boat. He had to take a picture of it before and after, so it was definitely not going to fall into anybody's hands. He had to burn that boat. There was absolutely nothing wrong with it. As a little kid I rowed that boat out there fishing all over the place.

Is the rowboat painted?
Yes. It had to be 40 coats of paint on it if it needed it or not. That was the old lighthouse way. Here is your paint. You had better use it too. But don't use too much. Don't run out. We spent a lot of time fishing. It was excellent fishing there.

What was the boat's original purpose?
We didn't have any buoys or anything to take care of there. It was for just around the dock. We used it mostly for just fishing. We did lots of fishing.

Campbell family photo

Dick with the lighthouse row boat

I see a picture here of a bobcat?
We had a dump. Our landfill was right back of the house because it dropped right off into nowhere. So for years we just dumped all of our cans and garbage over the side. One summer, when we got back there, my dad kept saying, " You know, there is some kind of animal here." It was strange because we had noticed that there weren't any rabbits. You saw how it dropped off. At different times my dad would say, "You know I saw something peek up over the edge of that." They were trying to figure out what it was. Then finally, watching closely, they said that's some kind of an animal, possibly a bobcat. So my father went to the DNR. They gave him a trap. They were afraid with kids around that whatever animal it was . . . and being out there in the mountain range. We got the trap. We caught him the first night. We set the trap just a little away from the house in the woods. We used rotten fish because that is what they said they liked to eat. It was a big leg trap. We put a long chain on it My dad and I went down there. Stop, look. The trap was gone. All the bark was torn off the tree. So right away we knew that whatever it was, was pretty powerful. He shouldn't have put the long chain on it. The bobcat went up the tree, he was trying to get away, and as he did he pulled the bark off.

Campbell family photo

The bobcat that that John Campbell killed. Notice that John got dressed in his keeper's uniform for this photo. Also notice plants next to the house entry.

And there he was, tangled in a limb quite high, tangled in that chain. After studying him a while my dad decided it was a bobcat. So my dad shot it. That was the end of that. There was only one. We were glad of that.

Did they get a gun as protection?
No, they had their own gun. I had a little rifle my dad had given me. That is what he shot it with.

How often did you see a tender?
Sometimes they would go on by, doing other things, but to stop while we were there in the summer, only twice. Usually the inspector came with the supplies. These were not supplies to eat, just to maintain the station.

What about work crews?
The one that seemed to be in charge and came to Huron Island most of the times was Ed Tormala. He came from somewhere in the Duluth area. He did all kinds of work. I don't know if he was an engineer. He would come there with two or three

others. He would do the carpenter work. He would stay for maybe a week or two at a time. We knew them real well because they would stay with us, eat their meals with us. It was like one happy family.

Do you remember Stewart Edward, he was an electrician?
He was an electrician? I know what he was there for then. He must have been in that crew. Down in the far end of the island, where the fog signal was, they had a lot of electricity for the air compressors and the LORAN system. It was a big building. They had a generator down there that ran constantly. Well, up the hill we

Campbell family photo

Dick and his dad taken in Pellston where the family stayed during the winter for a few of the years

had just two small Leroy gasoline generators and a battery bank that was worthless. It was old, outdated, and didn't work very well. You could run the generator and run directly off of it to get light. Lots of times that is what we did. It would run all night and during the day we would turn it off. The crew that came there, they ran wires from the far end of the island all the way up to the main tower. They came with a load of pipe that looked like small telephone poles, 2-inch pipe. They had an air compressor and they would drill holes in this solid rock and put in posts. It looked like a miniature power line that went twisting through the rocks all the way up to the main light. Then the electricity could come from that end of the island to the main light and eliminate this mess we had at the top of the hill. They were there for quite a while doing that because it was one hell of a job. They had to carry everything. It was a long, drawn out job. After they got the pipes and the posts in, then they had to string the wire. It took quite a while to do it. It was a hard job.

I've heard different stories about how you got supplies. What was the process?
I think it is that way today with the government, everything is backwards. You don't get what you ordered. Of course, your keepers and crews were rated on how much you used. For instance, if you used 100 gallons of oil, why are you ordering more this year? And if you could cut back on it, that was a feather in your hat. It was really tight. You've heard all those stories about paint brushes and stuff. You didn't throw anything away.

What about vacations there?
Usually it was taken in the winter. In the early days in the lighthouse service my dad had all winter off, except once in a while they would call him to Detroit to work at the lighthouse depot.

When you first started you could hear messages on the radio. At some point you had the radiobeacon and radiotelephone.
I don't remember when. Later years was when the radiobeacon was installed. They had the same thing here (Old Mackinac Point). It was a big mess. Big clocks, Seth Thomas, with the pendulums. Twice a day they had to make sure that radiobeacon was set right. They would tune in on a radio and get the signals from Greenwich Mean Time. It had to be within so many seconds. They were monitored several places on the Great Lakes by some Federal agency. If you got off more than just a few seconds you were reported and there is another big black mark. But it was very important that it was that way because in the fog these ships relied on those seconds. Five seconds could be a long way with a ship. It was very important that it be done that way.

What was your recollection of how that worked?
Each station had a different dot and dashes at a certain time during the 24 hours. During the fog they would turn it on continuous. Every 10 minutes, or something, it would emit these signals. It was really crude back in those days. They had a little light on the radiobeacon and when it would click on, the light would flash and show the dots and dashes. You could sit there and watch it. And you could hear it also. It was really crude back then. Anyway, the radiobeacon would send the signal out. You've seen what they call the radio direction finder on a ship, that funny shaped thing in the pilot house? On the ship they could turn their finder on and it worked almost like a radio. Suppose they are here in the Straits. Old Mackinac Point had one. Mackinac Island had one. Different ones in the area. They would turn that on and turn that direction finder. They would get the signal from here and from there and here we are. It was really reliable actually, especially in those days. If you were a few seconds off, it wouldn't coincide with this one over here. If this guy was right on the money and that guy over there was off, or not working at all, that was another thing – you had a power failure. You had to scramble to get that thing going there and get it set back right.

Could you run it by hand?
Oh, yeah. They might monitor you right at that moment. Then in the log book that had to be reported. Why, when, what time it went off, what time it came back on, who worked on it, what you did to it. Boy, I tell you. At the time, you think this is kind of silly. But it isn't. Suppose there was an accident.

It was probably a big deal?
Oh, it was a very big deal. Radiobeacons weren't there when we got there. But the radiotelephone showed up . That was pretty crude. It was so unreliable. It was the old tube type with things going wrong. You had to be a radio technician also because, along with the radio, they sent a whole car load of repair manuals and pieces, tubes, whatever, wave detectors.

What was it used for?
You could call a lot of stations or ships if there were any in the area. If you were lucky you might get another station.

What were you calling them for?
They would call in to say everything was OK, or there was an accident or somebody got sick or they needed something. But they had certain times when everybody would tune in and talk. You could do it in between. There was one station, I think it was Marquette, that monitored it all the time. Reliability was terrible.

The radiobeacon, what was the antenna like?
The one at Huron was a wire stretched between two big poles. The one that was at
Old Mackinac Point was a big steel tower. It was the same system that Huron
Island had. It was very effective. They did a heck of a job. They had to because
they were monitored constantly.

Do you remember the clocks that ran it?
I had one and like a fool I sold it. It was in this garage out here and the roof leaked
and it was going to get ruined. I had to sell. I get sick thinking about it. It was a
Seth Thomas clock. Big pendulum.

So when you got there this was a fully electric station?
Yeah, with our own generators.

The fog signal was powered by electricity. So your dad had to understand electricity.
There were quite a few things that he had to understand. Maybe they didn't understand it but they used trial and error enough to keep it going.

So the light was electric?
Yes.

Did it have a Fresnel lens in it?
Yes. But it flashed.

You had an electric bulb?
Yes. It flashed, It didn't rotate.

Did you ever go up in the tower?
Yes.

What was up there?
The lens. But those remote stations, they got a little lax about keeping them up.
They know that they would not be checked. There would be times that dust would
get on them. My dad would never let me touch it because those fingerprints on
there – oh no!

Sandy Planisek

Old Mackinac Point

What were the curtains in the lantern room like?
I recall at Huron Island there was a rod and they were black. I can't remember what kind of material they were, couldn't have been plastic. If I remember right, you could take them down and there was a rack that you could hang them on. It was a flat piece of material. One piece on each window.

At a lighthouse where an inspector would be looking at them quite often, they had to be real careful about that light. But up there, when they knew there wasn't much to worry about, there were days on end where they wouldn't bother doing anything. We were so remote, "Oh well." They wouldn't cover the lens or anything. Just about the time they figured they would have a visit, they would clean the lens and start using the curtains.

They say that part of it was to keep from having a fire.
That was just a part of it. They got dirty real quick if you left the curtains off. When they didn't use the curtains, it was quite a job then to start over on the cleaning after a week. The dust would settle and stick on there.

What did they use to clean with?
I'm not sure any more. I think the different guys had different ideas of what to use.

Did they wear an apron?
I never saw that. I know it was quite a job to do it. Time consuming. But it was important to do it. It reflects much better when it is clean.

Did they ever have trouble with the windows in the lantern room breaking?
Up there I do not recall that. But they used to leak a lot because of driving winds. There would be water blow in around them.

We never had any problem. We had enough ventilation to keep it dry and nice in the tower. It was all dry and white washed in there and beautiful. The stairs, that is stone right from that island.

Old Mackinac Point
1944-1958

How did he go from Huron Island to Old Mackinac Point?
Somebody retired from the station down here. He put in for this. Of course he did get it.

What was he looking for?
A shore station. I think my mother pushed that mostly. This was the best that we
ever had. We could all be together. Go to school. Be together every day.

When you came here to Mackinaw City, how old were you?
Fourteen years old.

What did you think about Mackinaw City vs. Huron Island?
It was a strange world. Of course the tourist business wasn't as big and great as
now. It was nice.

Were there things you missed? And things you appreciated having?
Good example of that, one time before we left up there my father took me into a
soda fountain in L'Anse. He bought me a chocolate malt. It was the first one I
ever had in my life and I thought there was nothing like it. It was the best thing in
the world. It was so creamy and great. I can remember that. I thought, where have
I been? 12 years old?

What did you miss?
It was a little more strict here. We had to keep things more in order in this station.
Because we were on land we never knew who was going to drive in and look the
place over. You know all about the inspections. It was probably worse than a
military inspection. Our shoes had to be lined up under our bed. That's the way it
was. Believe me, it was! It might not be for other lighthouses but it was for mine.
They had to be with no dust on them. Lined up just like in the army. In the closets
everything had to be hanging. Just like in the military. No boxes of junk. Nothing
stuffed under the bed. Beds made. It reminds me so much of being in the army.
There was no excuse for it not being that way. You had a little bit of time to run
around and straighten it up but major things, as you women know, you can't do it
that quick.

In inspections there would be four or five guys show up at once. One took care of
the machinery. One took care of the building and grounds. They all had their clip
board and they all walked around and graded you. They didn't tell you at that time
how you fared. They didn't tell you anything. You got your letter back later. That
was it, and it went on your report card of course.

My dad was really good most of the time. He always passed with flying colors on
almost any lighthouse except once, I can remember. One time. This was to show
you how crazy they can get. It was this lighthouse right here. He had scrubbed the
kitchen ceiling and painted it. Well when the inspectors came, later he saw the
report, the next time he paints the ceiling make sure he brushes it all in one direc-

tion. They could see brush marks. Apparently, my dad said something to him that made him mad, so the guy had to write something up bad about him. My dad is a lot like me, he was liable to tell them anything. Like I said, be careful with me because if something doesn't sit right . . . My son is the same way. I guess we inherited that or something.

As a kid was there anything that was worse here?
No, it was fine here. Everything was nice.

What about your dad?
He probably enjoyed it more than anyone else. He got involved with quite a few things. They were always involved with the veterans groups. Not necessarily the Legion. But he was with the VFW. They used to go to all the conventions around the country and veterans organizations.

What could you kids do here that you liked?
I didn't do much more. I had been away from sports and things like that, so I didn't play basketball.

Did you know what those sports were about?
Not too much, no. And I really didn't care. My interest was gone. My wife says I was somewhat of a renegade. We grew up together as kids. But she taught me. I can confess to this. I probably wouldn't have graduated from high school if it wouldn't have been for my wife. She kept me in school and did a lot of my work.

Did you find it strange being in a town?

Especially 12 months. We used to have a lot of visitors. We had a lot of room and all of the relatives used to come. Being up north, you know how it is. That was nice. We got relatives that we hadn't seen in years, or maybe never.

How many times did you see the inspector here?
Different times, different inspectors. One might be there just for the machinery this time and later on somebody else. It was spotty.

Sandy Planisek

Old Mackinac Point detail

John Campbell in uniform at Old Mackinac Point

Campbell family photo

A lot of the inspectors were really nice people. Over the years my dad got to know them. They knew him and the way he operated. Some of them would just walk in and say, "Hi John." Do the paperwork and be gone.

When he got here what lamp was in the tower?
We were hooked up on electric, sewer, water and the whole works. This was really nice. No outhouses. The fog signal was electric.

No generators?
They had an emergency generator in there. It used to come on. We used to have a lot of power failures years ago. What was nice, at meal time he could come in and eat and not have to be out at the fog signal.

When you were in Mackinaw was the barn here?
The so-called barn was made into a garage – two car garage. It had a ramp to get up into it.

There was another building?
Not when I came here. There was a playhouse, but it didn't belong to the government. It was the Marshall's. But they left it there on the back side of the garage. It was big enough that an adult could get in there easily.

Picket fence?
When I was there the picket fence was just around that tall tower that was there. It was a steel tower for the radiobeacon on the lake side of the fog signal building. There was a white picket fence around that – maybe 30 feet by 30.

When he was here, how many other people were here?
There was Olsen, my dad, the other civilian. It bounced back and forth. Rudy Stiphany, he was in the Coast Guard, stood a watch. Those three guys were the main ones when we came here. Of course they had to have somebody for the day off. They had some Coast Guard people running around here. They lived in a rooming house over here. The government paid them a little extra for their room.

Your family and the keeper's family shared the big house?
Yes.

Did they keep this light going 12 months?
Yes, it was year-round. One thing, because of the ferries. There wasn't much chance of anything happening, but back then, there wasn't any navigation other than the railroad ferry. Later years they started running the tankers through here.

Did they do watches here as well?
Yes, year round.

Did you have a vacation of so many weeks off?
Yes. They were really strict about that too. As a kid I tried to collect things like kids do. That was not allowed. My Dad made me get rid of anything.

Fishing?
A little bit. I didn't do much fishing here until after I was married. Her father and I used to fish right out front here.

Your dad didn't have time to fish now, or he thought people were watching and he couldn't fish?
Well, I suppose he didn't have time. And he didn't have to. We never did much recreation fishing. We did commercial. Strictly to eat or sell.

What did he do for recreation here?
I don't know. Hunting. He got involved in other things. A bugle corps in Harbor Springs. He was a bugler in that for years. They were always busy.

How about card playing?
They used to do some, but I don't remember them doing much up there. I know they did at a lot of places. They used to play cribbage. Martin used to cheat all the time. My dad was always jumping on him for cheating. We had a battery radio but the batteries were always dead.

How about reading?
Lots of reading.

Did you get one of those library boxes?
If they requested it. Sometimes they got it and sometimes they didn't. But you usually had to request it. There was usually one sitting there, but whether anybody used it, I don't know. They didn't do that here.

Newspapers?
Out on the island, no.

When you were here your mother probably bought the food in town?
Yes, they never did furnish any groceries or allotments. No where.

How much did your dad make?
I don't remember. It would have been Coast Guard wages. He came here in '44. That is why they bounced him around in the U.P.

The uniform changed when it went from lighthouse service to Coast Guard. Did he have to supply his own uniform?
I don't know if he got an allowance when he was in the lighthouse service or not. I don't know the story behind that. But in the Coast Guard it was like any military. They allow you the first one, and so much once in a while to replace it.

Did he wear his uniform all of the time? At any of these places?
No. He wasn't one to wear a uniform. He didn't flaunt it. He had been in WWI and he had these overseas ribbons. All of his lighthouse time counted. So in some of these pictures he has all of these hash marks and ribbons. He would go somewhere involving the Coast Guard and the lighthouse and they would say they have a veteran here. That is one of the things that got him through the inspections. He is an old-timer, leave him alone.

Nancy – His pay was around $2300 when he started. He got to making around $4,000 for the Coast Guard. The way the cost of living went toward the end he was certainly not keeping up.

At some point Henrik Olsen retired and your dad was appointed keeper?
Yes, 1951.

What did he say about that?
He knew his time here was coming to an end with the building of the bridge.

Old Mackinac Point fog signal

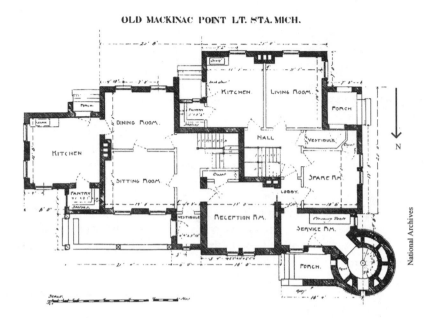

OLD MACKINAC POINT LT. STA. MICH.

Even in '51 he knew the bridge was in the making?
Yes, he knew that sooner or later it was going to happen. He was getting up in years so he really wasn't worried about it. Then he had the chance to go to Betsie. He liked Betsie. That was a nice station.

Did you go there?
Not to live. But we visited there lots of times. I was married by then. I was in the service part of the time.

Can you tell us about the rooms at Old Mackinac Point and what happened where?
They lived on the east side. The kitchen is where it is marked (on the floor plan). The dining room and sitting room – they show a partition there which was not here when we got here. Stairs went up and one went down. We called this big room our living room. Wide open all the way across.

Did you eat in the kitchen?
Yes, we ate in the kitchen. We had a dining room table. The reception room was my parent's bedroom. Off of that was a door that you could go to the tower. Both

sides could go to the tower without going through the other. This was our big porch across the front. Two bedrooms on our side overlooking the fog signal. And a bathroom.

What colors where there?
It was what my dad called shit brindle. It was a brindle color – brown or something. The Coast Guard came up with light pea green. Trim was varnished. Our kitchen was all wainscoted with oak and varnished, the doors and all around the doors. And plaster.

They would come through and say how much paint did you use in this room? They had it right down to practically the ounce. They would keep track of that. It came mixed. Some of it came in square 5-gallon cans. You better have enough to do it, and you didn't have any extra either.

Did your dad like this job?
I think he did. In later years when the pay didn't keep up. . . But most lighthouses weren't made for winter, this one was cold in the winter. It had this big steam boiler. Not insulated. Double brick wall. Terrible. When the wind blew it was

Sandra L. Planisek

Pt. Betsie

terrible. You ordered a car load of coal. It would arrive in the fall, it varied from 50 to 60 tons a car load, train car load. A contractor would haul it. We would put what we could in the basement – big coal bin in the basement. The rest of it they dumped outside next to the fog signal. In the spring we would be lucky to make it. Of course we each had a cook stove and the fog signal had a coal stove in it. That was a fraction of what that boiler used and you just about froze to death. Every Saturday my job was to haul clinkers out. We had clinkers you would not believe. I had to haul clinkers and ashes out. Every night, when I came home from school, I walked in the kitchen door and there was the kitchen range my mother cooked on, a terrible thing. My job was take that ash pan out of that range. It had to be emptied every day. You pull that thing out and there is dust and dirt. My mother would make me put newspapers down. That wouldn't help much. There were always two bucketsful in there. You would pull the first one out and take it and dump it and then come back and get another one. You had to shake the grates down, every day. Then you had to haul in two scuttles full of coal and a little bit of kindling wood to start the fire in the morning.

What were your dad's duties?
There was quite a bit of goofy bookwork out in that fog signal. They had to keep track of all that foolishness. Why and what-for log books, supplies. They had a couple of different books. One was for the machinery in there. The other one was a general log. In the general log they would say fog signal on at such and such, off at such and such.

That served as the office?
The office and machinery was all in one. In the end of the building was where the radiobeacon was. They put a little partition across there. That is where the lens is now. That was another cold, old building. The fog signal was heated by coal and you had this big old, brown colored, coal heater, square. Great big stack on it. You notice the chim-

Point Betsie

ney is real high because the draft down there is terrible when the wind blows. It was so cold in there that, when it would get down below zero, they would sit there with their pea coats on, a watch cap down over their ears and mitts on, and they would get right next to the stove with that.   Right against the stove and sitting there with their boots on to keep warm. That's how cold it was in the fog signal.

Being the keeper he had to keep the biggest part of the log. Some times he would let it go two or three days at a time. They finally got a telephone. The only phone down there was in the fog signal. When the Coast Guard kids were here he spent most of his time chasing them around, trying to make sure they stood their watch, getting them out of jail and things like that. Sometimes they would even run away, go awol. There were monthly reports, weekly reports, daily reports. The weather bureau had a little thing down there too. They took the temperature. They kept a record of it and once a month sent it in.

Pt. Betsie
1959-1963

What was it like at Pt. Betsie?
He liked it down there. It was all Coast Guard except him. He was the only civilian. He lived in the lighthouse on the keeper's side. A Coast Guard lived on the other side. I took my wife and two boys down there one time. Southwest winds on Lake Michigan can get really wild. This was Nancy's real good experience in a lighthouse. Pt. Betsie has jetties across the front. When you get a southwest wind it comes straight in. It was freezing, around Christmas time. We slept in the upstairs bedroom on the southwest side. I don't think she slept. In the morning ice was all over the whole lighthouse and driveway and everything. You could hardly open the door. Everything would rattle. He really enjoyed it there. There was a nice Coast Guard that worked there with him. There was a Coast Guard station in Frankfort, down in town. He did know those guys.

He retired from Point Betsie and died shortly after on August 23, 1963.

What was the job like at Pt. Betsie?
It was almost identical to this. You know how close the fog signal is to the house? He spent a lot of his time in the house.

How do you feel about the fact that you were a lighthouse kid?
My father being a Native American, we lived on the "rez" up there. I've seen the other side of life. I know about prejudice and a lot of things about that. Now, with our economic situation, I don't want for anything. If I want something I go get it. But back then it wasn't that way.

There were times when I thought it wasn't good, but overall today I think it was good. I don't know what would have happened if I would have been out in a social life like most people grew up in. I don't belong to any organizations. I don't really care too. My ideas are quite a bit different than most people. I watch television. I read the papers. I have my own views. I sometimes get myself in trouble for expressing them. We are all getting old. You have a lot different ideas than other generations.

I could move to an island and it wouldn't bother me in the least. In fact, I would enjoy it by myself. Leave me alone. But maybe if I would have started out young on this other life it might not have been that way.

In the beginning, fishing with dad at Grassy Island

Campbell family photo

Grassy Island

Grassy Island Lighthouse was Dick Campbell's first lighthouse home. During the interview Dick mentioned that the light and, in fact, the island no longer exist. I wanted a photo of this light and began a search. Immediately it became clear that Dick's home actually was the front range light of a range light set.

MaryAnn Moore, a GLLKA educator, visited Wyandotte's Bacon Library and found several photos identified as Grassy Island, but none of the photos looked like the pictures in Dick Campbell's album. Further searching revealed that there had been two Grassy Islands, each containing a range light set. MaryAnn went to a metropark on the river which had maps of the changing islands over time and drew us this sketch from the time period the Campbells lived on Grassy Island. The Campbells evidently lived on North Grassy Island.

While researching lighthouse history, MaryAnn also found some interesting news articles from an old newspaper, the *Wyandotte Herald*.

GLLKA Board member Terry Pepper has a lot of information on the lighthouses of Lakes Huron, Michigan, and Superior. Unfortunately, Terry has not collected information on the lights of the Detroit River. However, Terry did provide the detailed reports on the lighthouses conducted by the lighthouse service in 1909. These reports were obtained from the Coast Guard.

Even with all of this information it is difficult to distinguish the Grassy Island lighthouses. Check the information yourself and see if you can figure out which is the rear light. Remember that the front range light is always shorter than the rear range light.

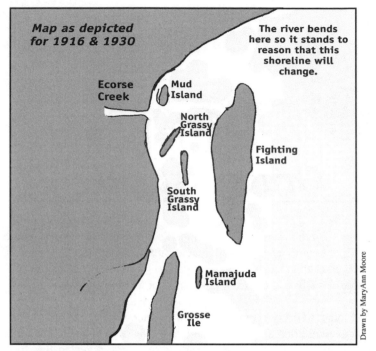

*Comparing this map with the modern one in Dick Campbell's chapter
you see that Mamajuda Island and South Grassy Island no longer exist*

~~~~~~

Wyandotte Herald, January 28, 1881, Vol III, No. 5   pg. 3
*"A new lighthouse on Grassy Island is contemplated. The foundation has been made and
stone and lumber is being hauled over the ice to the island preparatory to building it next
summer."*

~~~~~~

Wyandotte Herald. Feb. 18, 1881 Vol 111, No. 8   pg 3
*"A Bay City servant girl fell into a cistern, recently, in which was a hole cut in the ice, with
the water some four feet below it. Her head and shoulders went through the hole, but her
hips stuck. When she was missed, after a few minutes, a pair of legs were frantically waving
above the ice in the cistern, and a smothered voice below was calling on various saints. It
took several neighbors to get her out."*

~~~~~~

Wyandotte Herald, November 16, 1888, Vol X, #46   pg. 3
"Captain John DeSana was after the job as lighthouse keeper at Grassy Island before the election knocked out his calculations galley west. John M. Bryan will probably continue in the position."

> *Funk and Wagnalls Standard Dictionary* 1898
> Galley west: slang, to destruction or confusion; as his
> coming knocked their plans galley west.

Wyandotte Herald, January 24, 1890   Vol XII, No. 4 pg. 3
"John M. Bryan, keeper of the Grassy Island light, was in town on Wednesday, shopping. Mr. Bryan said he experienced some difficulty in crossing the river on account of the floating ice - the first time he has been troubled that way this winter. He is keeping "bachelor's hall," Mrs. Bryan and the children living on this side during the cold weather, so that the children can attend school. Mr. Bryan takes his isolation philosophically and finds company in his dog, pipe, his own books, and a library of 36 volumes furnished by the government."

Wyandotte Herald, October 9, 1903
"Charles Boston is engaged in driving piles at Grassy Island, so that a house can be built for the keepers of the range lights at Ecorse. The light on the island must remain while the house is being built, and it is moved out of the way daily, although it weighs about ten tons. At night, however, it must be placed back on the same line with the other light in order that the boats traveling up and down the river can steer by it."

North Front Range Light

General

Name of station .... Grassy Island North Channel Range Front Beacon
Date of report 2/1/1909
Inspector .... Chas. Bartlett, Chief Clerk & Norris Works, Supt.
Location .... In 3.5' of water, near N'ly end of the flats, lying to N'd & W'd of Grassy Island. W'ly side of main channel of Detroit River.
Latitude .... 42° 13' 45"
Longitude: .... 83° 08' 09"

Premises

Site area .... Area of land about dwelling & tower is about 92' x 171' = 15,732 sq. ft. 0.36 acres
Landing .... Small landing on Easterly side & small landing along boat way.
Access to station .... By row or sail boat from Ecorse, MI., about 1 mile.
Distance to nearest road ... Ecorse, 1 mile
Distance to Post Office ..... Ecorse, 1 mile
Distance to village .... Ecorse, 1 mile
Public conveyance .... To Ecorse, by L.S & M.S. RR or by MI Cent. RR or by electric car.
Private conveyance .... Row or sail boat from Ecorse to station about 1 mile.
Means to support lantern .. Tower on dwelling
Number of lights .... one
Established 1897
Tower shape in plan .... Square
Base to ventilator ball .... 28'
Focal plane (mean water) .. 30'
Tower color .... light straw, white trim
Color produced by .... paint
Tower connection .... connected, projects from NE side of rectangular 1 story dwelling.
Object of navigation .... Range light. Detroit River Channel.
Building material .... wood
Wall thickness base .... 8"
Wall thickness parapet .... 8'
Tower base diameter .... 11" Tower projects slightly from front of dwelling.
Tower diameter parapet .... 11"
Stairway & steps .... circular, wooden hand oil finish
Number of landings .... None above 2nd floor of dwelling
Size of glass .... 14" x 20"
Number of windows .... 3 windows, 2 lights each 14" x 20"
Number of doors 1
Foundation .... Combined tower & dwelling foundation of brick, resting on piles.
Ground character .... clay
Soil susceptibility .... grass
Miscellaneous remarks .... Embankment between & area about beacons, which was thrown up when the station was built, was extensively repaired when washed away & otherwise injured in 1900. At front beacon, there is a good growth of grass, with sev. fruit trees in bearing.

Lantern & fixtures

Order of lantern 4th
Lantern shape .... polygonal
Diameter .... 6' 10"
Number of sides 8
Number of plates each 1
Plate thickness .... 1/4" or 5/16"
Size of plate .... 31 1/4" x 36.5"
Storm panes .... None

Unglazed lantern side .... 5 - 225 degrees
Lantern construction .... wood
Roof construction .... Wood, covered with copper & lined with zinc.
Ventilator / cowl............... copper
Lightning spindle .... copper, platinum point
Lightning conductor........... 3/8" solid copper, led down outside of tower into
moist earth
Railing .... Wooden balcony covered with copper, iron pipe railing
Lantern doors .... Double wooden doors, 1 swinging out & 1 swinging in.
Lantern floor .... Wood, hand oil finish
Watch room door .... Door from 2nd floor of dwelling.
Gallery diameter................. 6' 6"
Ventilator location .... 6 brass, revolving
Ladders .... none
Curtain hooks .... Brass, screwed into lantern posts

Illuminating Apparatus

Marks & numbers .... A. No. 6
Order of apparatus .... lens lantern
Inside diameter .... 11 13/16"
Characteristic .... Fixed red
Arc of each panel.............. 90 degrees visible between Bearing S 18 - 04 E to S
71 - 56 W; Azimuth 161-56 to 251-56; 45 degrees
each side of range
Number of panel 1
Prisms above center 3
Prisms below center........... 3
Pedestal .... Octagonal wooden, forming newel post of stairs.
Service table .... Wooden, over stairs, shelf underneath
Draft tube description .... Painted, galvanized iron tube, over lens lantern
How color produced .... Ruby chimney
Lamp type .... 5th order
Number spare wicks........... 2
Number spare burners 2
Lamp type .... Single wick
Diameter outside wick .... 1 1/4"

Closets & Store rooms

Tower closet use .... Good sized closet in 2nd story, fitted with shelves &
table for lamps, etc.
Oil house description .... Square iron oil house NW of dwelling, fitted with
shelves for 5-gal. cases.
Other storage areas........... 3 small storerooms in basement
Suitability .... Suited, dry

Dwelling

Location .... Attached, tower rises in NE face of dwelling.
Color .... Light straw, white trim
Construction materials ...... wood on brick foundation on piles, with good cellar
having cement floor.
Number of rooms .... 4 rooms, pantry, office attic & 3 rooms in cellar
Number of keepers 1

Outbuildings .... Ice house, oil house
Outbuilding colors .... Ice house - light straw, white trim; oil house - dark red.
Paths & walks .... Cement with frame front of dwelling around side with main walk leading to rear tower.
Area enclosed .... None
Area of garden .... None
Timber or shrubbery .... A few trees
Cultivated area.................... None
Surrounding character .... Marsh

Water supply

How procured.................... River
Quality .... Good
Quantity .... Ample
Injury possible .... By storm
Purity precaution .... None
Tank capacity.................... None
Tank material .... From river by 2 iron pumps, 1 in basement, 1 in kitchen.

Miscellaneous

Landing.............................. Boathouse, 16' x 24' attached to S side of dwelling. Arranged so that boat may be kept in boathouse on rollers.

North Front Range Light

Bacon Memorial District Library, Wyandotte, Michigan

North Rear Range Light

General
Name of station .... Grassy Island North Channel Range Rear Beacon
Date of report 2/1/1909
Inspector .... Chas. Bartlett, Chief Clerk & Norris Works, Supt.
Location .... In 5.5' of water, 2000', S 26 degrees - 56 W in rear of Front Beacon.
Latitude .... 42˚ 13' 28"
Longitude: .... 83˚ 08' 21"

Premises
Site area .... Beacon surrounded by an embankment protected with rip-rap stones.
Landing .... Small landing on Easterly side & small landing along boat way.
Access to station .... From front beacon: by board walk about 2000' long, on embankment between the beacons.
Private conveyance .... Row or sail boat from Ecorse to station about 1 mile.
Means to support lantern .. Tower on dwelling
Number of lights .... one
Established 1897
Tower shape in plan .... Square
For of tower .... pyramidal
Base to ventilator ball .... 47' 9"
Focal plane (mean water) .. 50'
Tower color .... light straw, white trim
Color produced by .... paint
Tower connection .... Dwelling at front beacon.
Object of navigation .... Forms a range with Front Beacon for main channel,
.... Detroit River.
Building material .... wood
Wall thickness base .... 10"
Wall thickness parapet ...... 10"
Tower base diameter .... 15' 2" sq..
Tower diameter parapet .... 8' 7" sq.
Stairway & steps .... wooden, hand oil finish
Number of landings 3
Size of glass .... 10" x 12"
Number of windows .... 8 double sash, 4 lights to each sash.
Number of doors .... 1 double, swinging out & swinging in.
Foundation .... Beacon rests on 4 parallel concrete walls resting on piles.
Ground character .... marsh
Soil susceptibility .... yes

Lantern & fixtures
Order of lantern 4th
Lantern shape .... polygonal
Diameter .... 6' 10"
Number of sides 8

Type of bars .... Vertical
Height glazed .... 36"
Number of plates each 1

Plate thickness .... 1/4"
Size of plate .... 1 - 36x36"; 2 - 30 1/4" x 36"
Storm panes .... None
Unglazed lantern side .... 5 - 225 degrees
Lantern construction .... wood
Roof construction .... Wood, covered with copper & lined with zinc.
Ventilator / cowl .... copper
Lightning spindle .... copper, platinum point
Lightning conductor .... 3/8" solid copper & led down side of tower into moist earth.
Railing .... Wooden balcony covered with copper, iron pipe hand rail.
Lantern doors .... 1 double, swinging in & swinging out.
Lantern floor .... Wood
Watch room door .... None.
Gallery diameter .... 6' 6"
Ventilator location .... 4 in parapet wall, with brass revolving discs
Ladders .... none
Curtain hooks .... Brass, screwed into corner posts.
Watch room .... Floor below lantern fitted with small table, with enclosed shelves, door & corner shelves.

Illuminating Apparatus
Marks & numbers .... 3 No. 9
Order of apparatus .... 90 degrees lens lantern
Inside diameter .... 11 13/16"
Characteristic .... Fixed red
Arc of each panel .... 90 degrees visible between Bearing S 18 - 04 E to S 71 - 56 W; Azimuth 161-56 to 251-56; 45 degrees each side of range.
Number of panels 1
Prisms above center 3
Prisms below center 3
Pedestal .... Wooden octagonal, also serves as newel post at top of stairs.
Service table .... Wooden, over stairs, shelves underneath
Draft tube description .... None
How color produced .... Ruby chimney
Lamp type .... 5th order
Number spare wicks 2
Number spare burners 0
Lamp type .... Single wick
Diameter outside wick .... 1 1/4"

Closets & Store rooms
Tower closet use .... 1st floor fitted with large closet under stairs.
Oil house description .... Oil stored in sq. iron oil house at Front Beacon.

Which of these lighthouses is being described in the report as the North Rear Light?

Michigan Lighthouse Conservancy

Michigan Lighthouse Conservancy

Bacon Memorial District Library, Wyandotte, Michigan

Campbell family photo

Hint: This is not Grassy Island, but it is John Campbell on the scaffolding

Grassy Island Today

From the Bacon Library, Local History, Detroit River

"Wyandotte National Wildlife Refuge
US. Fish and Wildlife Service

History of the Refuge

Grassy Island appears as a 6-acre marshy area on 1796 maps of the Detroit River. At that time, the river bottom around the island sloped gradually off on all sides into deeper channels. The area was called 'Ile Marecageuse' on the 1796 map and 'Grassy Island' on later maps. An 1873 fisheries report contains a line drawing of the "Grassy Island Pond Fishery" for spawning whitefish. The drawing depicts a large seine being drawn in by horse-drawn windlasses and several sheds on the island. The fishery employed 30 men, working night and day, September to November and produced 45,000 adult whitefish per spawning season.

An executive order in 1843 reserved the islands for lighthouse purposes, and navigation lights have been on the island for years. In 1955 Grassy Island was under the jurisdiction of the U. S. Treasury Department, which had reserved it for installation of navigation aids by the U.S. Coast Guard. In September 1959, the U. S. Army Corps of Engineers began diking the 300-acre area around Grassy Island for disposal of polluted dredge spoils from the Rouge River.

. . .

In January 1960, Mr. Dingell introduced legislation to designate Grassy Island and surrounding shoals as a national wildlife refuge because wildcelery (*Vallisneria americana*) was abundant and widely distributed near Grassy Island. Wildcelery is the preferred food of diving ducks, such as canvasbacks, redheads, and scaup. In July 1960, the Department of the Interior agreed that if it received jurisdiction over the Grassy Island area, it would not object to the continued use of a 72-acre Grassy Island Confined Disposal Facility for dredge spoils from the Rouge River. . . . "

Grassy Island Fishery   Note the lighthouse on the left.

Bacon Memorial District Library, Wyandotte, Michigan

4

Helen (Campbell) Nakarado

Daughter of Keeper John P. Campbell

Interviewed January 7, 2004 by Sandy Planisek and Dick Moehl

You might expect that Helen Campbell, older sister of Dick, might have had quite a different lighthouse experience being a girl. I expected to hear more about the household duties, more about the difficulty of life for the lighthouse wife. I did hear some of this, but far less than I expected. Starting as early as 1932 it appears that the girls had basically the same experiences as the boys. They romped with the boys and worked along side of their father.

One explanation might be the division of household duties between the father and mother in a lighthouse keeper's family. The father assumed some duties that today we might consider the duties of the wife, such as painting the interior of the house, cleaning some parts of the house, as well as repairing the house. When pressed Helen points out that her mother was not overly busy at the lighthouse. She cooked, washed and cleaned. All other tasks fell to the men.

Helen did talk more about her mother than Dick did, but perhaps I asked more. She called her mother adventurous, adaptable, content, and fun. Being the sole parent of six kids for six months of the year must have been a challenge but Helen did not sense that her mother felt burdened.

Helen was older, age five to nine, during the period of family life on Grassy Island but does not have more memories of that time. She grew up during the family's eight years on Huron Island. By the time the family moved to Mackinaw City, Helen was 17 and almost graduated from high school. She spent very little time in Mackinaw. Her memories are primarily of Huron Island.

Helen and Dick's memories of shared events differ only slightly. Helen did not appear to have been forced to act as a little mother watching over the smaller kids. All of the kids were free to roam unsupervised. She was free to be herself and she is the only lighthouse child we interviewed who relished the library box.

Although all of the lighthouse kids, Campbells and Collins, played together, they did so as neighbors. Helen made it clear that three separate families lived on Huron Island. They did not act like one big family. The kids might play together one day and not the next. The men maintained separate housing even when the families left the island. Because "standing watch" occurred at the remote fog signal building, the men did not see much of each other either. The Campbells left Huron Island before the Collins' did. The kids went separate ways. The kids did not remain life-long friends and only recently have rediscovered each other.

Helen left the world of lighthouses with her marriage and professional career. She has only recently returned to the Straits of Mackinac. She did return to Huron Island with her sons and thoroughly enjoyed it.

Do you remember where Grassy Island was?
When we went there I was five, so as far as the location of things it is pretty much of a blur. When we went to the shore to live it was in Wyandotte.

It was during the depression. Living there my dad would row my sister and me across to the mainland for school.

How far was that?
It didn't seem like it was a long way, but a little girl can't remember.

Can you remember what the name of the school was?
My dad would row us in. That was during the depression so there were docks there with houseboats, old rickety houseboats. People lived there for a cheap place to live. He had made arrangements with an old couple in case he wasn't able to get there to pick us up in the afternoon. We could go to their houseboat and stay. We, me and my older sister, would go there and we would take a bus to where the school was.

Did you spend much time on this houseboat?
No, he always got there. I remember some foggy mornings when it was kind of different going because it was a little scary. He had one of those old fashioned

metal horns that you could blow in. I don't know how much good that would have done. But he would stop and listen so we wouldn't get run over in this thick fog. Blow into the horn and then keep on going.

He was concerned about larger boats between the island and the mainland?
Evidently. Yes.

What are your first memories of being at the lighthouse?
I remember going. It was during the depression time and my dad had not been able to get a job anywhere. He had come home from the First World War and worked at various things and then took the test for this. He went down ahead of us. My mother brought Dick and me and my sister. Dick cried the whole time; he was just a baby. My mother was a real adventurer.

Where were you leaving?
Harbor Springs. Both of my parents were from that area. My mother for a couple of generations.

Do you remember your grandparents?
Oh sure. My great-grandmother, Rebecca Ann Bennett, was from Greenville. Her husband left her with small children. Her brothers had a sawmill close to Boyne Highlands, close by what is now one of the ski resorts. They had her come up and cook for them. Her brother would take care of the children. Later she moved into town. She lived at the base of the hill when you went into Harbor Springs. That was her house. She had my grandmother and my Aunt Helen and Uncle Glen.

That was when there was diphtheria around and they didn't have anything good to take care of diphtheria. Some people had died of it at a cottage at Harbor Point. The house was just closed up and left for some time because no one wanted to live there. Finally someone bought it and wanted it remodeled. So my grandfather Hammond and another man, a carpenter, took the job. They both got diphtheria and my grandfather died. So my grandmother Hammond was left with little children. Her name was Diadama Geneva Hammond.

So my great grandmother and my grandmother built a house on the main street of Harbor Springs out of an old ice house, where they had stored blocks of ice they cut in the bay. That house was there until just a few years ago. Very recently I went by and someone had built a big house there. Then Grandma married John Wright and lived on the top of the hill.

Helen (Campbell) Nakarado at the interview

Richard L. Mohel

They had what children?

My mother, of course. She married when she was about 18 and her husband went into the First World War and died of the flu. She had a son named Ronald who was a year old when his dad died. Then my dad came home from the First World War and they had been sweethearts before. (Laugh) A romantic story. They married. My mother's name was Edna. There are not very many good pictures of my mother. Somehow she was always caught scrubbing on the scrub board or sitting in an unflattering picture. She was a very pretty lady.

John and Edna's wedding photo

Campbell family photo

What about the other side of the family?
The other side is more difficult, I can't go back very far. My grandmother on my dad's side married a couple of times. I guess she was pretty popular too. My dad had just one brother who was much younger than he. I hardly knew my grandfather on that side because they got a divorce when I was young. I saw him a few times but I never had much to do with him. My grandmother was one of 15 or 17 kids. So my dad had cousins strung all over. We would go somewhere and he'd wave to somebody and we would say, "Who is that"? He would say, one of my cousins. We never believed that you know. How can anybody have this many cousins? But I guess it was real.

Where were you born, in Harbor Springs?
Yes.

Your parents both grew up there?
My dad went to school there some, but he lived in Cross Village and on a farm out of Harbor. But my mother had always lived there. The Hammonds had a flower shop right on the main street of Harbor Springs. How can we know all of these stories because no one did what you are doing. I would never have dreamed of asking my grandmother personal questions. That wouldn't have been done.

She was that strict?
No, that was just the way it was then. Kids didn't intrude that much.

My mother told me about wearing these black sateen bloomers. That's what they wore for sports. They wore these black bloomers. And then they would be cold and they would back up against the stove and they'd burn themselves because of those hot pants.

Campbell family photo

Helen in swim suit

Then your dad took this test?
He couldn't get a job. He had a job with the city but he received a pension of $7 a month because he had

been wounded in the war. He had worked a short time and someone objected because he had an income. So he got fired because he received $7 a month. That was not enough to live on. He had been doing all sorts of things to make a living. Being a veteran, I guess with Civil Service you got a break in getting a job. He took the lighthouse job and went down there. Of course they were very much in debt because they hadn't had a very good income for a while. When they first went down there they used to send most of the money back to pay the bills they had run up.

Was his first lighthouse service job at Grassy Island?
Yes.

What did your mother think about that?
I don't know. She was probably glad that he got a job. My mother was pretty adaptable. She did very well.

He actually moved in and then you came down?
Yes. He was the assistant keeper. There was a keeper there named Mr. Lewis.

Did Mr. Lewis have a family?
Just a wife and a dog.

Which part of the house did you live in?
I don't remember. It was very nice. I doubt that it was new. The house stood on a small square. It had a big yard in the front. But it evidently had been man-made

Mrs. Lewis, Helen, Mrs. Edna Campbell, and Dick with dog Jerry at Grassy Island

because it was very squared off. Evidently there had been dredging done to create this. Behind the house the island had a long tail on it. It went a long way out and it was marshy. We never went out there because it was just marshy.

It was during prohibition and we used to sit out on the front of that house and watch the rum runners from Canada. You would see the authorities chasing them. It used to be quite exciting. That was our entertainment. But one time the authorities were getting close to this one that had the liquor. The rum runners came around into this area where it was all reeds and shallow water. They dumped what they had in the reeds. Of course my dad was watching. Then they left. The authorities circled around but they didn't see anything. So – my dad liked to drink of course. The next morning he is out there with a pike pole trying to find those cases of liquor. He tried a lot. My mother was so afraid. "John, what if they come back? They will shoot you for taking their liquor." He never did find it. It was pretty exciting. I can remember watching him from afar.

Campbell family photo

Is this your boat?
Yes. They had to patrol up and down the river to check the buoys every night to see that they were operating. It was a pretty fancy boat. It wasn't too practical. This is dad. He always had some kind of little

Grassy Island Lighthouse

Campbell family photo

Keeper Lewis' dog Jerry greets John Campbell as they approach the dock

hat on. This was not a very practical boat because you would go boom, boom (banging on waves), as you would go up and down the river. We thought it was pretty nice.

Let's look at this picture of the back of the house. What are these buildings?
I have no idea.

Was there an outhouse?
I don't remember.

This looks like a barn.
It was like a workshop as I remember. This is where they pulled the boat in, the boat house. I remember there being a workbench. This was basement on the side. It was a work area.

HELEN - MRS LEWIS on scow in back of House Grassy Island

Campbell family photo

Back of house

Things would float down the river?
In fact they pulled some mattresses out of the river, at least one mattress. They used it after it dried out. I don't think the river was as polluted then as it is now. It sounds horrible. My mother heard Dick crying one night. She got up with a flashlight to see what was wrong and there were bed bugs biting him. The moral of the story is you don't pull a mattress out of the river. You have to remember how poor people were at that time. You bought shoes for $1 a pair. They would wear out and we would put cardboard in them. It was a bad time.

Did you have much furniture?
No, we didn't have much furniture. I don't remember any moving van or anything. We just went down in a car. I don't have any recollection of what was there. That is probably why the mattress got pulled out.

I showed her newspaper articles.(See end of chapter)
I remember the *Marigold*. I have no memory of a tender coming there. I remember going shopping for groceries.

Campbell family photo

The Campbell family, Dick and John, Edna and Helen on the mattress

Did your parents get a cash allowance?
No I don't think so. I think they got paid a small amount once a month. It wasn't much. Of course no one got paid much then.

Do you remember any talk about disease?
No. We didn't swim there I know. We went in the water some when we went to Wyandotte. I remember running around the yard in a bathing suit.

Do you remember what you ate? What you did in your spare time?
I don't have very many memories of any special things. We had company. People would stop by in boats. Sometimes strangers would stop and look around. I can't tell you very much about what we did. Just kids stuff I guess.

You lived on the island year round?
Yes.

You were able to get to school?
I don't remember any stories of not being able to get there. We had to take a bus. It must have been a city bus because you had to pay a dime to go on it. My older sister was supposed to take care of me and we would go together. So I had my dime, but the teacher was going to have some activity where you had to buy this little flower watering can. It cost a dime. I spent my dime on the watering can. So

I didn't have any money for the bus and my sister had to walk with me many blocks to get back to where we had to go (laugh), with her hollering at me the whole time because she had to walk too.

When we lived in Wyandotte the school that we walked to was quite a few blocks away. At that time there was a program in Michigan for dental care. They put up dental chairs in the schools. These students would come and work on your teeth. We didn't have any money for our teeth so my parents signed the waiver to have us worked on. In one day they pulled all my back teeth, my second teeth. It made me so sick. I remember having to sit down on people's lawns because I was weak from all that. From then on whenever I would go to the dentist as an adult they would say what a crime that was that they did that to me. They must have been practicing extractions.

What about eye care?
I don't remember that. We used to get them checked. I think some people on welfare got glasses. But my mother would never have gone on welfare. I think she would have starved first.

What was your mother like?
Ummm. Well, she was a good person. I have to think, I don't know what her strongest trait is. When you have six kids I guess that is your strongest trait. She was not an outwardly sentimental person. When my youngest sister finally went to school there were people there crying because their kids were going to school. My mother would just say something like, "I'm just so glad to have everyone gone. I can finally have a day of my own." We kids weren't close together. We were strung out over her lifetime.

How far apart were you?
My half brother is 10 years older and my youngest sister is 10 years younger. I am definitely the middle child. She was glad to have some time to herself. (Laugh)

I wouldn't say that she was outwardly sentimental or gushy. I don't remember her crying very often. I think she

Campbell family photo

The family moved from Grassy Island to the mainland in Wyandotte

was pretty accepting of her fate in life.   I remember her drying diapers out the window.

Do you remember her doing laundry at this place?
Not there. I don't remember.

Do you have any good memories of Grassy Island?
I don't have any bad memories. My dad was a very fun dad and we did lots of things as a family together.

Did he take you out on the boat?
Oh sure. We used to go with him on these trips checking buoys. We didn't spend too long there.

Were you proud of your dad?
Oh yes, yes.

Did the other kids comment on how lucky or unlucky you were?
No, they didn't even know.

Campbell family photo

Wyandotte house from the river

You moved into town. Which side did you live in?
Right side. My sister and I had bedrooms in front and my parents' bedroom was in the back. My second youngest sister was born in that house, Kathleen. It was a difficult place to live because we were very close to the main office in Detroit. The inspectors came often. How my mother endured it, I don't know. They were very, very strict. This was a brand new house, a brand new lawn and everything. There we were, little kids. When they would come unannounced there was never supposed to be anything out of place, anything dirty. Supposedly people didn't eat or something. They would write up the craziest things. We were taught never to touch the walls or the woodwork. We had to keep everything just so. We were raised that way. I would come home from school and change clothes into play clothes. They came one time and my shoes, instead of being lined up in the closet, were beside the bed where I had taken them off. Dad got written up for that. My sister, Kathleen, was born there. She was in the high chair eating. You know how babies are messy eating. Got written up for this messy baby with stuff around. There was a tree out in the back yard. He put a swing there for us. We started to wear the grass away. So he had to take the swing down because it wore the grass. We never had toys. We might have one thing because you couldn't have toys around. That wasn't allowed. It was a very difficult place for them to live being so close to the inspectors and the house being so handy to them. It was rather a relief when we got out to Huron Island. You could see the inspectors coming.

It was a beautiful house but I doubt if it had anything wrong with it when we left. Down the yard was the boat house and little workshop where they kept the boat where they still patrolled for the buoys in the river.

Your dad's main job there was checking buoys?
Yes, as far as I know.

Huron Island

Then you went to Huron Island?
Yes. It was really a big trip at that time because it was gravel roads, certainly no expressways or anything.

You didn't go by boat, you drove?
Oh, yes. Up to where we took the boat.

What did you own? Did you go in one car?
They had furniture of their own at that time. I don't remember them purchasing it but we had furniture when we lived in that house. I don't remember how it got there.

Of course going to Huron Island was not going to be a year-round place. It would only be during navigation season. So we moved to Harbor Springs actually, back to their old home town.

Did they buy a house there?
No, they didn't have money to buy a house. All the years that we went to Huron Island they would let the house go when they moved out in the spring.

They would just rent for a few months?
Yes, they would rent during the school year and then let it go because they didn't want to have to pay the rent. So every year they had to get a different house. We lived in a lot of different houses.

What did your mom do with your stuff?
I think she must have put it at my grandmother's there in the barn. I don't have a clear recollection of that. We didn't think anything of it.

Do you remember your first trip out to Huron Island? Was it an adventure?
Oh, sure. First of all it took a long time to drive from Harbor Springs up there. It doesn't seem like that long now, although it is still quite a ways. Cut River Bridge wasn't there. It was this gravel road that wound around over little bridges over that river. The whole trip was like that. We didn't have any station wagon or anything, just a car. We had to take everything, all our clothes and stuff, plus all these kids and the dog in the car. One time we had a flat tire. The trunk was just crammed. We had a flat tire. So dad couldn't get at the jack. I remember him getting a log and all of us kids sitting on the log to hoist the car up. I used to get car sick, that was always

interesting. My sister would get sea sick. So between the two, interesting trip.

Did it take more than one day?
We'd go at night because they had all these different ideas of how to keep me from getting sick.

Going at night was one of them?
Yes. There were all sorts of ideas that people would give them. One was putting a piece of newspaper on my chest. I don't know what that was supposed to do. (Laugh.)

So they wanted me sleeping in the back seat. It would be a long night. If we did go in the daytime we didn't have the money to go in restaurants. They would stop in a store and get some bologna and bread and some ketchup and we would stop and have some sandwiches. My dad liked to gamble. I remember where you come into a little bit of Wisconsin and they had gambling there. He would go in and gamble a little bit and earn enough. Once in a while we did go into a restaurant, he'd make enough money. He was so lucky. Do you remember those old punch cards they used to have where you could win a box of candy? You'd have to pay whatever it said on there, like a penny or whatever. They'd have them in lots of the tobacco stores. He was real lucky on those. So we did have treats some times that he would win.

You moved back to Harbor Springs. Did he go up alone at first and you come along?
Yes, we would be in school when navigation opened in April.

Did you go to school in Harbor Springs?
Yes.

You would drive up to Huron Island?
Dad would drive. Mother would have the car at home and he would come home on a train, or however he could get there, and go with us. We would go the day after school let out.

Where would you go to?
Skanee. The Falk Bros. had a fishing operation there and a dock. That's where the boat always went and tied up.

You would get on a government boat there?
Yes.

What was your first impression of this island?
Well it was pretty fun. It was really, really a wonderful childhood. It was just great. We had a wonderful time.

How about your mother? Did she think so? Did she worry about you?
Well I don't know how she came to her decision of how to let things go, but she pretty much let us have freedom. She trusted that we were OK. She would have had a nervous breakdown if she was going to worry about us. The first year that we were there we didn't stay all summer because she was pregnant. She had my youngest sister in October. So you could see she was very pregnant that first year. I think we probably stayed maybe a month.

So the next year my sister wasn't even a year old. She was creeping. My dad made a crib for her. He cut the little evergreen saplings to make the railings of the crib. When he made it he put them quite far apart. Our bedrooms were on the second story of the main lighthouse. The way that you went to the second story was around the spiral staircase that you went up. Our kitchen was in the little cottage next door so we only went upstairs for sleeping. My mother took her up to bed and stayed with her until she went to sleep and then came back down. It was daylight of course. My sister woke up, crept down that spiral staircase, and out the front door. There was a wooden walkway across the front which made the turn down toward the cottage. After she had made the turn my mother spotted her in her little nightgown creeping on this wooden walkway. When you've seen the pictures you know that it was a steep drop off the front. Had she tumbled over no one would have ever known what happened to her.

When my grandmother, who never went out there, heard about it, she was talking about tying ropes on the children. We had lots of freedom.

There we did have chores. We had a chart up on the wall of what we had to do in the morning before we could go anywhere. Once we were done with our chores we were free to do whatever we wanted. We could go all over this island because we would climb on rocks. Adults couldn't do what we did, so they never went where we went. We cut down trees. We built things. We had a lot of free time.

You didn't break any parts ever?
Never, the only thing I did was, while cutting on a tree, I think we were making a church, I cut my finger. Another time I cut my foot with a knife. It should have

Campbell family photo

The front door of the lighthouse leads to a dramatic drop to the lake. The baby crawled along the wooden sidewalk towards the white wooden house that held the family kitchen.

had stitches but of course there were no stitches then. They put bandages on and tied them up. I stepped on a nail once and it went into the ball of my foot. I had to have a piece of salt pork on it for quite a while. That will draw out stuff. One of the staples at islands was salt pork because it was salted. That was something that would keep. You could have meat and not have to worry about it. People still buy salt pork to make beans.

Talking about the rock out back.
Yes, everybody spent time there. That was sort of a meeting place. You looked toward shore and you could see Pt. Abbaye and a lot of things. It was a smooth rock and it had the bench there. You could sit in the sun or there would be a breeze. The one thing there was flies. Flies that bite. They were terrible. One of my memories at night was, before dad would go on watch, you would hear bang, bang. He would take the fly swatter and kill them before he would leave. You would be half awake. Oh, those flies were terrible on the whole island because there were all these places where water could lay. We didn't have mosquitoes. I only remember those flies and they were just part of the year. You can see how clear the water still is.

What were some of your chores?
Well, actually I don't remember what they were. I used to cook a lot. I liked to bake. We were always hungry because we spent all day swimming and playing. When we would come up to eat we were just starved. I liked to bake. I used to get into that quite a bit.

Do you remember what kind of stove you had?
Not a very good stove for a while at least. It was one of those kerosene ones with the different burners in it. A funny oven, one of those metal things that sit on the top. Have you seen a kerosene stove on a table top?

I'm sure we got a different stove later. I don't remember it. But I am sure we did because we made lots of cakes and all kinds of stuff, so I'm sure we used another stove.

You had to make a lot. We only went to shore every couple of weeks. Plus you didn't buy cakes and things. You made your own. There was a lot of cooking that went on. Only part of us kids were there, because my half brother and sister were older. My half brother never was there. My sister was there for a while and then she wasn't there. My sister Dawn was a baby. Mainly it was the Collins kids and Dick and I.

How many Collins kids were there?
Five. It was quite a group.

Were they there when you got there?
Yes. I don't remember that they knew much more than we did. We sure had fun.

Do you remember what happened in the different parts of the lighthouse?
This is where the generator was (back). The generator just ran at night for the light. It was not for our use. It was for the light.

Did it run all night?
Yes.

And you were sleeping in these rooms (back top).
Yes. And there was a cistern somewhere that caught water just for washing. We carried up all our drinking water. No one was allowed to come up without carrying a pail in each hand, even when you were little. You cleaned out the gallon paint pails and you had one in each hand. If you started playing and swinging them around and the water got lost you had to go back down and fill them up or you would be in trouble. It was just an accepted thing. You had to do that.

What did you do with the water when you got it up here?
I don't remember. We must have poured it into something.

How did you get upstairs?
We went upstairs from the front. Up the spiral staircase. As far as I know that was the only way to get up there.

The spiral steps must have had a door to the first floor and a door to the second floor.
Yes.

Campbell family photo

Mrs. Edna Campbell

Was there a hall?
I just remember one big room. But there could have been. Those photos with the dormers are more recent pictures. There weren't any dormers.

What happened in the white wooden building?
When we were first there we slept upstairs (in the lighthouse). Across the back of the wooden building was a room and that was our kitchen. The Peterson's, the third man that was out there, he had no children, he and his wife lived in the front part of the white wooden building. Later on we moved into the front of the white wooden. We no longer used the upstairs part of the lighthouse.

Were the Peterson's gone?
No they were still here. They had the back kitchen and evidently they must have slept in the big house. We must have just switched.

Looking at the picture of people at the wooden house.
Yes, that is Maud Peterson holding the baby. My dad is up on the ladder painting. That would have been Martin Peterson. He was Norwegian. He had a little accent. Nice people. So the kitchen we used was in the middle windows on the side.

The wooden sidewalk spanned the uneven rock. Notice the glacial striations in the rock. Something as simple as putting up a clothes line required ingenuity in this environment.

The front was a living and sleeping room. It ended up that we had bunks in there. There was a bedroom on the far side where my parents slept. The kitchen was on one side, the bedroom on the other. It is still like that.

Did you get to go back?
Yes, not last summer, the summer before (2002). My boys had always wanted to go. I kept saying no, no, no, I don't want to go. So finally, a year ago last summer, they chartered a couple of little boats and we went.

Did you have a good time?
Wonderful. We spent the day. There were so many things that were the same. The flowers that were growing, the flax, the lilies, the roses. Same spots.

Looking at the picture of the island.
This is facing toward the big part of the lake. The signal is down here off to the left.

How far do you think that was? How long did it take you to walk?
I don't remember. I would guess a mile. It is not a very big island but it is very up and down and rocky.

That was the paint thing (oil house). It was on the path to the boat house. I don't remember it. This is the outhouse. Did Dick tell you about walking in his sleep?

The light station was perched on the highest rock formation on the island. The view was spectacular but the walking was dangerous.

How many holes were in the outhouse?
I think there were two and a kid one. It was a wonderful outhouse. They had to keep everything perfect even there. It never smelled. It probably had, who knows, how many coats of paint on it. It was like satin. That gray paint that they used. Get painted once a year maybe more. Lids on them. I don't remember ever shutting the door. You would gaze out.

The boardwalk continued on beyond that outhouse. They didn't throw things over there anymore when we were there. But evidently they had in the past. So when Dick walked in his sleep he went out this way. When he walked in his sleep we watched him walk right over the end of that. He didn't even wake up. He got up and came back in and went back to bed. In the morning when he got up he said, I don't know why I'm all sore mother.

Do you remember them cleaning this out?
The outhouse? Heavens no. But there had been an old dump where they had thrown trash in the past. Dick probably told you about sitting there. It was my dad who saw the bobcat.

Do you remember where you washed your clothes?
In my old album, the one I can't find, I have a picture of my mother with her wash tub right about here in front of the cottage with her wash board and the tub. That's one of those wonderful pictures of her with a kerchief on. Really we didn't get very dirty. It was not a dirty place. It is rock and all.

I thought she might take them down to the water and do them.
No, no, no.

Campbell family photo

The walk between the boat house and the lighthouse as seen in 1900. Today the walkway is concrete with pipe railing.

Too far away?
Yeah. She never went down there. I doubt if she went down there ever. It was down a rocky cliff thing. She mainly just went on the trails.

You're going to the boat house there. This is the back of the house. Up in this area (under the foot bridge) was full of tiger lilies. Down in this area was phlox. It was real pretty there. That's still there.

Somebody planted those?
Yes, must have been many years ago.

If you were going to go out on a typical day where would you roam off to?
We would go swimming every day, down by the boat house. That is what we mainly did. There wasn't a good place to swim at the fog signal. It was very deep and steep. There was a little dock. Occasionally we would go down there and we would get dad to swim with us. Off from that were some rocks that you could swim to. Maybe twice a year we would get him to dive in and swim out to the rocks. But otherwise we swam down at the boat house. The first of June when we would get there we would start wading and our legs would be blue and red. My dad would swear at us. He was always swearing. Jesus — — there was ice in here last week. That was probably true. But we would keep doing that until we got used to it. Then we would swim the rest of the year. People would come out there from Huron Mountain Club and we would dive for a quarter. Just like the natives somewhere. They thought it was really something that people would go in that cold water.

It is really something.
I had talked about it so much that when we went there both of my sons had to dive in and see if really was as cold as we made out it was. I have pictures of them in the water. Of course the water is beautiful out there still. It is so clear. It was cold but they had to argue a little bit about it.

Dick remembers going out in the boat a lot. Do you remember going out in the boat?
We weren't allowed to use the boat in the first place because it was part of the operating stuff. But, when they replaced this boat and got a different one, dad said we could play with it. So we did. What happened, the government being as it is, when they decide to replace something, whatever they are replacing has to be destroyed. If it is a refrigerator or whatever it had to be destroyed. They don't

give it away or anything. I don't think anyone ever knew who reported it but someone evidently reported that the boat hadn't been destroyed. So Mr. Collins got a message that they had to burn it and they had to take pictures of it while it was being burned to prove that it had been destroyed. Here we are way out in the lake, what does it hurt letting us kids use it? But while we had it we had a wonderful time. We both remember going down on a very windy day and getting it pointed into the waves off of the boat house and just having a wonderful time with it. Just keeping it headed right. We are not very far away from the boat house in which they had installed phones by then. The phones were on the island just at three spots. We could hear that ringing. It was an old one, a crank phone. We could hear that ringing and ringing. They looked with the binoculars and saw what was going on. So we got in a little bit of trouble with that. Occasionally we did get in trouble. It was never all that serious.

What would be the official government purpose of a boat like that? Not to go to Skanee?
No, no, no. It was just for around there. My dad used it to troll for fish that we ate every day, rowing it. I don't know. . . I guess they figured that you would have to have some kind of boat like that. What if someone was in trouble and you just needed to get out?

Maybe it had something to do with the tender?
I have a picture of the tender here some place. I don't know which one it is. They would go into the signal and unload there because they had the barrels of oil. Later on they put a pipeline in because the oil was necessary for the generator for the light.

They could pump it right from the boat?
No, they put it into tanks.

How often do you think the tender would come?
I remember it coming at least once while we were there in the summer. Of course it would come and pick them up in December. That's how they got off the island.

They usually stayed until before, or after Christmas?
Navigation would usually close before Christmas. I think it always did. Probably about the middle of December. It would be pretty stormy by then. So they would get picked up by one of the tenders and brought into Marquette usually.

Then you would pick him up there?
My mother did. Or he would take the train down. He would be home from then until navigation was going to be open again in April, about the middle of April, I think.

We talked about Stewart Edward working there.
I remember two Coast Guards spending most of the summer, maybe all of the summer, putting in the pipeline. One was an Indian from Oklahoma, a great big fellow. And the other was from Boston. The one from Boston was homesick, so homesick. Being out there. They were both young. I was maybe 14 or 15 years old, old enough to be interested in boys. That was kind of fun for me, made the summer go faster.

Stewart Edward remembers your dad. When I said Huron Island he said, "Yes, Johnny Campbell." He remembered the bobcat story.
That was an interesting time.

Was anyone regularly at the boat house?
No, we were pretty regularly there. People think it is pretty strange with boys and girls both, with these Collins'. That boat house was built so the boat was recessed. The concrete coming up, it was higher at the one end than the other. So there was just this space where the track was that they winched up the boat. We used to have peeing contests, girls and boys. To pee across that. (Laugh)

I'd think the boys probably won.
Well, when you are young you can do better. (Laugh) We made our own fun. We had lots and lots of fun.

Would you be gone all day? Did you take a sandwich?
No, we would go back up. Kids don't think anything of running

Huron Island boat house photographed in 1991

Campbell family photo

up a trail. One of our other escapades, where Dick got in trouble, was (he probably tells this differently) there were still a lot of trout fishermen. The Falks, and other fishermen too, fished all around the island. They had nets set. So we decided that we should go raise a net one evening. So we went around to the front side of the island and raised a net and took out a few fish and put it back. We got back and it was getting dark and so we started up with these fish. We thought we were special, we caught these fish. Oh, was my dad mad! Owww! Because the fishermen were our friends. Well, before we got up there Dick got scared. He threw away his fish. We kept ours and took them up. I think that Dick was in more trouble than we were because he threw away that fish. But then I remember us being grilled about it, you know. "I suppose you tangled that net all up." And Dick saying, "No, no, we were really careful we put it back just like it was. It is not tangled." I think we probably did do all right with it because we'd seen enough fishermen. I don't think anything ever occurred, but I think my dad had visions of these fishermen being angry that somebody messed around with their nets.

Did these fishermen come to the house to visit some times?
When it was stormy they would come in that spot . . . Down near the boat house was a little island that had a little fish shack on it. In stormy weather, or whatever reason, they would stay in that shack. They were safe in there.

Where would they put their nets?
They had nets all around. There were lots of fish then. That was before the eels.

The boat that took them back and forth to Skanee. Notice the two kids' heads in the portholes. John Campbell is standing in the door.

Did they come out of Skanee?
Yes, the Falks did.

Did you see the inspector very often there?
Not too often there. The only time they came was when the tender would come.
We could see that coming, so there were never any dirty dishes because we would
have everything done before they could get up. In fact I became famous for my
cakes. So they would have some baked goods.

How many inspectors would come?
I remember two.

Do you remember how they worked?
They weren't bad. They were pretty friendly. Especially since the same ones were
coming all the time. It was easy to do. That little cottage, you could see all over it.
The signal was always immaculate. The men kept everything just so. It wasn't
like being down near the main office. Plus, probably, changing times.

Do you remember many maintenance crews coming?
I remember putting in the pipe. Other than that I don't remember a lot.

Steward Edward said they just ate with the family.
Probably, they couldn't cook and there wouldn't be any place for them to go. So I
am sure they did.

He left the impression that they didn't pay or bring food
That might have been true. We wouldn't have thought very much of it.

Except if money was tight.
That's true, but we ate fish every day. That came out of the lake. Dad fished. We
baked everything.

Did you have chickens?
No

You bought eggs and milk?
We had to use canned milk. We didn't drink much milk in the summer. I didn't
like canned milk.

Campbell family photo

(From left) Helen, Kathleen, Dick, and Diana Dawn with their dad

Did you look forward to going into town?
Oh sure, I used to go with my dad lots, probably more than the other kids. He stood watch from 12 till 4 – noon till 4 and midnight till 4, except when someone was gone. Then it was 12 till 6. So we would leave when he got off watch. First we would stop at Skanee for a little bit and then we would go on into L'Anse to buy groceries. He would have a grocery list from all of the families that were there. That was a real big thing to do. So we go to the grocery store. Then our next stop was the ice cream parlor. My dad loved ice cream. I remember they would be getting the syrup out and they would be sweeping the floor because it would be in the morning, when you didn't usually sell much ice cream. We would go back and finish up with the groceries. Then there used to be a bar about half way between

L'Anse and Skanee. So we would stop there and dad would have beer. So he would drink the beer. Then we would go back and load up all the groceries. This little boat had a cabin but it was really a roly-poly boat. By then he would be getting tired. We would head out and then he would have me take us home. He would lay down. There used to be a bench along the side. He would lay down on that bench. So if it got too rough this roly-poly boat would start rolling too much and he would start to roll off the bench. Then he would get up to see how things were going. That was the routine.

Did you like doing that?
Sure. Sometimes it would be so rough with this little boat that the waves would go over the top so you couldn't see. You had to use the compass to get there. Then you would have to hang on real tight to the steering wheel because you could fall on the engine and get burned. The engine was right there.

Did the compass work well up there? Was there iron?
It worked well.

Was there anything you had to watch out for?
No, it was all deep. You were protected in the bay to begin with coming out. As soon as you got beyond the point, Point Abbaye, it got rough.

Does a river come out at Skanee?
No.

In good weather you could navigate by sight?
Sure.

Did your dad do most of the going to the grocery or did they take turns?
They took turns. Often times one fellow would be on his week's leave and so you'd have to pick him up.

How did that work?
They got a week each month but dad never took his because we lived so far away. We just stayed there. One year we did go and tented and took a trip. That was pretty thrilling for us kids. During the war, when he got put in the Coast Guard and had to spend the winter at the station at Keweenaw, we lived in Baraga. He had to stay at a Coast Guard station during the winter. But he would come home on his day off to Baraga.

Dad did wear a different uniform during the war. When he had to be in the Coast Guard he had to wear a Coast Guard uniform.

Did he go away during the war?
No, he was still in the lighthouse service. In the winter time he had to be at Portage Entry, in the Keweenaw. There was a Coast Guard station there. That is why we lived in Baraga that year. Because he stayed at Portage Entry. He was in the Coast Guard. They made everyone be in the Coast Guard. When the war was over he went back as a civilian. He was a bosun's mate first class.

So you went to school there?
Yes, at Baraga. We were there the last year that we were on the island. I was 17 then. That last summer I didn't stay out at the island. I stayed mainly in Baraga. I had a little job working at a little telephone office there in Baraga. I was the night operator. So I only made a couple of trips out that summer.

When he had vacation and he stayed on the island what did you do?
Nothing, you just lost it. If you didn't leave you were working.

Did he like his job?
I guess. I think about him so many times and compare him to modern young men and think of all the things he didn't get to do. He rarely got to go to weddings or graduations or special events because he would be there. He missed many things.

How many brothers and sisters did he have?
Just one brother. So he pretty much spent his life taking care of his family, being a dad.

Did you have any people come to visit you at Huron Island?
No. It was a long trip at that time.

What would you do when it rained and you couldn't go out and romp around?
Rain, that wouldn't stop anybody. We probably played games, cards. Whatever kids do.

Did you read?
Oh, I read all the time. They would deliver a wooden crate of books from Detroit. It would be in a crate so when you opened up one side it was like bookshelves. It would have a whole assortment of books. That was my thing. I read everything. All of the books in there. Whatever they were.

Then you would get to order another batch when you finished reading them?
No, it would take all summer. There were a lot of books in there. And you didn't just sit and read all the time. I probably was the reader of everything. I used to go and stand watch with my dad a lot. I would do some reading then too.

Did you pick up magazines or newspapers from town?
I'm sure the adults did but I don't remember doing it. I'm sure they did because that would have been a pretty interesting time then.

Library box

Could you have had toys there?
We could have had except we didn't. For one thing, I don't know where we would have gotten them or where we would have had the money to get them. Our big event all summer was 4th of July. We were allowed to look through the catalog of fireworks and pick out a set of fireworks. We would spend a lot of time with that. They would buy us each a pop and a watermelon. 4th of July was a big thing.

You got to buy the fireworks?
Yes. Those little rocket things. And we would have pop and watermelon.

Were birthdays a big thing?
I don't think any of us had a birthday. On dad's birthday we used to have a birthday cake.

Any of the Collins kids?
We had lots of cake. Mrs. Collins made wonderful cakes. I have some of her recipes written in a book somewhere. She used to make good cakes too.

Was it sort of like one big family?
No.

Everybody cooked separate?
Oh, yes. The families were on good terms but not real close. The adults weren't.
There wasn't a great deal of going back and forth, of people sitting around. There
was a lot of work to do and people stayed separate. I think that was probably
necessary too. You couldn't be that close. You couldn't live too close and get
along well with different personalities. I don't remember there ever being any
problems. We didn't have any problems as kids with fighting or anything either.

*Because the men stood watch the men probably didn't spend much time with each
other.*
Not really. Especially when one would be gone. They would just meet on the trail.
This Martin he was getting old and all he talked about was the weather. After dad
was there for quite a while it was getting pretty hard for Martin. In the fall with
Mr. Collins gone, with just the two of them there and with no one else to talk to and
bad weather, dad would say, "All that Martin would say is, 'well the thermometer
dropped so much.'" Or the barometer or whatever. In fact when he (John Campbell)
got to transfer the inspector came and said, "I think you have been here long enough."
He had the opportunity to go to Mackinaw City then.

Was it a good family life?
Um-huh. We had a really good time. The only thing was, you would never know
it now because I am really gabby, but through that whole summer of just being out
there we would get so shy that we had a little problem when we would come off of
the island going and talking to other people. That was back before supermarkets.
There in Mackinaw was Liebecks old store where you went in and asked for what
you wanted at the counter. So my mother would pull up in front and tell us to go in
and get a loaf of bread or milk or whatever. We'd argue with each other – you go,
no, you go. We were afraid. We were scared to go in there and ask for a loaf of
bread. It would take us awhile to get over that. But it was good. Really good.

*You did end up moving to Mackinaw even though you had moved out and gotten a
job?*
No, no, no, that was just a little job. I was a junior in high school at Baraga. Then
we moved to Mackinaw and I would have been a senior but I couldn't go to school
because they didn't have all the classes I needed. So I sort of went back and forth
to Pellston. I graduated from Pellston High School. So, I never went to school
there but I lived there.

How was that lighthouse and the life there different from Huron Island?
Oh, lots different. No comparison.

Better or worse?
Just different. For my time of life it was excellent.

Because there were boys?
Sure. But then I went away to school. I didn't ever live in Mackinaw the way Dick and my younger sisters did because of being older. I don't know all the people they know. I was married there at the lighthouse.

Did you marry someone from Pellston?
No. I just went to school there that year. I married a fellow working for Western Electric. I went to work for the telephone company in Petoskey. I went into nurses training for a year but I didn't like it. I was very homesick. I think that living like we did made me more homesick. Being in an entirely different world it was really hard. So I came home and went to work in Petoskey. But I was married right there at the lighthouse.

Did you get back to see your grandparents now that you were close?
My grandmother, my mother's mother, spent a lot of time with us. In fact, she died in the lighthouse. When she was ill they brought her there. She had never been in the hospital in her whole life so she went for a day or two and she had tests. There wasn't anything they could do so we brought her home. I helped my mother take care of her.

When mother put the girls in school she put Kathleen in the wrong grade. Pretty soon the teacher said she seems to know everything. It was finally discovered when the records were transferred that she was in the wrong grade.

How did your mother feel about the life style? Did she look forward to going out there for the summer?
I guess so. It was just an accepting thing. For one thing she and my dad would get to be together. There was a long period of time when they weren't. She was really a fun mother because all that period of time, when my dad would be gone, she would think up fun things to do. We'd go on picnics. She'd pile us all in the car. We would go and spend a day on the beach or pick wildflowers or cooking or whatever. We had lots of fun with her too. She didn't put housework ahead of fun.

When she moved off the island she didn't have to worry about everything being perfect.
Yes, that is true. There really wasn't that much pressure on the island because the men took care of all the painting and washing walls. All of that kind of stuff.

Always did, in Mackinaw too. A lot of women take that on as their job. Because the building belonged to the government the men did all that. At the island we didn't have much furniture. There wasn't a lot of dust. It would blow away if there was. The kids were gone swimming most of the time. I think she enjoyed it too. I'm sure it was tough some times. The laundry was a job but, like I said, we didn't get that dirty either.

I don't remember hearing when she died. I remember hearing that your dad died at Point Betsie.
He didn't die at Point Betsie. He did move. They moved to Harbor Springs and bought a house there. He died there. My mother died in 1975. She was 75. She was born in 1899. Both my mother and dad were born in 1899. It was easy to keep track of how old they were.

Did she every talk about which place she liked the best?
I don't think so. But of course when she moved back to Harbor Springs she still had the old friends from her young time. People used to keep friends their whole lives. I think she enjoyed being back in Harbor Springs. Sort of picked up after all those years. And it was all familiar to her.

Most people didn't move around that much. She would have been unusual having moved and moved.
She spent a lot of time in Harbor Springs in between. We'd come back there and go to school.

Most of those years you went to school in Harbor Springs?
I went there through junior high. Then they bought a house in Pellston and they would come back to that house. We lived in a big wonderful farm house. It was a mile from town.

She didn't have to deal with the lack of modern conveniences most of the year?
No. I think she liked it. I don't remember any fights or sadness or anything.

Which lighthouse was the best for you?
Probably Huron Island for my childhood. There was something that I never did until I was an adult, I never learned to ride a bike. There was no place to ride a bike. After I was grown I had to buy a bike and learn to ride it. I missed out on that. I never had girl friends from an early age. I was the middle child and more by myself. We never spent a long time at a school. I had friends, but. . . I see people who went their whole life long and have life- long girl friends. You traded one thing off for another.

The Campbells were on Grassy Island from 1932 to 1936

May 16, 1890 *Wyandotte Herald.* Vol XII No 20, pg 3. "The keel blocks for the government lighthouse tender *Mariold* are laid and the iron to be used in her construction has commenced to arrive."

Wyandotte Herald July 29, 1932
"Swimmers Warned Against Bathing in the River"

As a result of an informal conference participated in by Mayor Arthur W. Edwards, William P. Rutledge, chief of police, Health Officer Pasternacki and City Engineer D. C. Conway, it was decided to post signs warning people, adult or juvenile, from swimming in the Detroit River.

One case of typhoid fever, which caused the death of a boy, was traced directly to bathing in the river. The untreated water is unfit to drink and unfit to swim in. Danger from typhoid infection is so great as to make the warning necessary."

Wyandotte Herald Sept 17, 1936
"Board Hammers at Pollution Detroit River"

" . . . Wyandotte doesn't have to look far backward to recall an epidemic that for a time at least threatened to close our borders in a strictly enforced citywide quarantine - the infantile paralysis epidemic of last summer. The condition of the river may not be positively blamed for that epidemic, it is true, as the medical profession advise that without having isolated the germ they are uncertain whether same be dust, wind, or water borne. Therefore we, in Wyandotte, would be entirely justified in believing that the contagion came originally from the cesspool which formerly was the Detroit River."

Finding Huron Islands before the Lighthouse

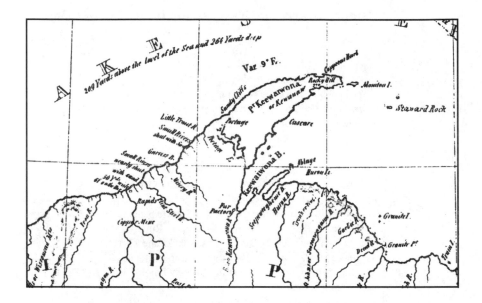

"There are three brothers of the Stanords, all captains upon Lake Superior; Charles, Benjamin, and John, who have all been for more than ten years there, and are the oldest and best pilots, careful and good seamen, and gentlemen. John, who is master of the schooner *Swallow*, has come to be called the 'pig let out of a bag,' from the fact that after running for days together in the dense fogs without land or bottom he scarcely ever loses his 'reckoning' and if he does, he fires a gun, and by its echo he knows if he is near land – and if so, determines by its vibrations the coast he is upon, and thence how to shape his course. So too with the brothers. Long years of experience in feeling their way with the gun, enables them to judge of the land when the sound rolls along it, although they cannot see it, with an astonishing certainty. This occurred after being three days in a fog without soundings or sight of land. "All quiet," said Capt. John, "till we ascertain if land is near, and where we are; it ought to be pretty close – fire!" The blaze opened the thick fog before the gun; the sound rolled over the water for a second, then a crash! Another – another – then the sound rumbled along to the eastward. "I thought so – the Huron Islands – did you hear it rattle among the mountains, and then roll along the shore to the north-east."

A True Description of the Lake Superior Country, St. John, New York, 1846, pp. 27-28.
Charles C. Stannard was the discoverer of Stannard Rock Reef.

5

James E. Collins

Clayton and Jim Collins, sons of Keeper James Edwin Collins

Interviewed January 14, 2004 by Sandy Planisek and Dick Moehl

Dick and Helen Campbell's Huron Island stories always included the five Collins kids who lived on Huron Island while the Campbell family lived there. Dick gave us the phone number of Clayton Collins and we scheduled an interview at Clayton's home in L'Anse, Michigan. Both Jim (J) and Clayton (C) were at the interview so as you read the following pages you will see both of their answers. The conversation transported them back in time more fully than any of the other interviewees. They laughed together, completed each others sentences, and talked as much to each other as they talked to us. This interview was great fun to do even though we, the interviewers, drove through a blizzard, and slipped into a snow bank getting there and arrived in L'Anse to find the schools closed.

Clayton has a quick sense of humor and you have to read his answers closely. On occasion he is having fun with his brother or me rather than giving a straight answer. He also has an interesting accent and even as I read these words, months after the interview, I can hear his speech, his timing, as well as visualize his expressions.

The Collins' tell about events they remember. Thus they have no stories from Detroit River or Stannard Rock. Unlike Dick Campbell, who works to keep his family's history and stories alive, these fellows grew away from their history in their adult lives and only now are returning as a result of the restoration of the Huron Island Lighthouse.

Another notable difference between the Campbells and the Collins' is that the Campbell kids tell about spending a lot of time with their dad. The Collins boys do not. Also, Mrs. Collins is seldom mentioned. There were five Collins children of similar age and they spent time with each other, thus probably not seeking as much time with their parents.

Despite the adage that "old men have bad memories," it is interesting to see how closely the Campbell's and Collins' stories match. All of the Huron Island kids remembered the tennis shoes, bobcat, the amazing rowboat, and stealing fish from the commercial fishermen's gill net. It is interesting to compare and contrast the different perspectives of these notable events.

The Collins boys spent more of their growing-up years at Huron Island than did HelenCampbell (Nakarado). They are so thankful that their dad took them to this place that changed their lives.

Your dad was born in Brimley, Michigan. What was the family business?
J - They just had a farm.
C - Just lived on a farm.
J -Lumberjacks and lumbering. Farming.

How did your dad get into lighthouses?
C - He wanted to go to work with his brother down in Detroit. His brother talked
him into it. More security. Of course he was born and raised close to Point Iroquois.
That's only four miles from Brimley. I guess that gave him some interest in it.

Did his brother set him up to take the test?
C - No, he just told my dad to get into something that's got some back to it.
J - He was in the army for WWI about three months. After he got discharged,
somehow or other, he got to do some schooling in navigation. Did it on his own. I
don't know where he got books to study from. He took a civil service exam. I
guess he passed the exam. That's from what I know about it.

Did he go to Detroit to take the exam?
J - No, I don't think so. That was his first station though. He was on Detroit River.
That's where mother and dad had their honeymoon.

What did he do on the Detroit River?
C - He was in a lighthouse there.
J - That was his first station.
C - Detroit River Light

Your folks got married in Detroit?
C -I think so.
J - I never saw their wedding certifi-
cate.
C - I've got it someplace. (Laugh)
J - He couldn't have been there too
long. Then he transferred up to
Iroquois Light.

*So his first lighthouse was the Detroit
River Light. Do you have any idea
what he did there?*
J - Second assistant, I think.
C - Second assistant, yeah. There are
usually three men at that time.

Detroit River Light

Did he ever say why he did that?
C - I think he just lucked out that there was an opening.
J - He advanced from second to first assistant at Iroquois Light.

Do you know what year he started in the service?
C - Was it 1919?
J - I think it was.

Right after the war?
C - Yes, right after the war.
J - It was a short time after.

Point Iroquois
1920?-1931

You don't know what year you went to Pt. Iroquois?
C - I didn't go there. My dad went there. I was born there. Marjorie was born in '22.
J - They must have gone there in '20 or '21. He did have that one season or two seasons in Detroit River. They must have had room for a family at Detroit River.
C - Oh, no, that is nothing but a tower.
J - That is where they had their honeymoon.
C - You don't need much room for a honeymoon. Just a little room that's all.

Most of you were born at?
C - Three of us were born at Point Iroquois. Marjorie, James and me.

What do you remember about Pt. Iroquois?
C - That was the first place I got a fish hook in my foot. (Laugh) They had to run me all the way into the Soo in an old Model T to take the fish hook out.

You stepped on it?
C - Yes. Somebody, my uncle or somebody, had dropped it in the grass. I said I'll find it. I found it all right. (Laugh)
J - The first time I saved his life was at Iroquois Light. He was standing out in front of the lighthouse with a hammer and 22 bullets. He still had a diaper. He was pounding 22 bullets and binging them around and I hid around the corner. Every time I made a run for him, he started pounding on another one. I'd run back.
C - I can still remember that too. (Laugh)

In your diapers you can remember that?
C - I don't think I was in diapers.
J - Yes, you were in your diapers.
C - I can remember him. He come around the corner looking to see what all the noise was, and I hit one, and away he went. I can still remember that. I don't know where I got the idea.

Where did you get the bullets? Did keepers normally have bullets?
C - No, they were up on a shelf in the back entrance in the light, in our apartment.
J - Dad had a 22.
C - I got up on a bench and I reached. I can still remember getting them off that shelf. I can't remember myself being that tall. I must have put something else under me to reach that high. Sometimes when we had caps they wouldn't go off in the cap gun. So we'd take a hammer and hit them on the cement. I think that is where I got the idea.

What did you do at Pt. Iroquois? You must have fished.
J - One spring they had a huge storm and they had a big ice shove, down to the mouth of the St. Marys River. Ice went clear across to Canada, high icebergs. There were icebergs that formed along the dock by Iroquois Light. The signal was right along the dock. My dad and Mr. Byrnes, who was the keeper, were together in the signal making herring nets. They fished for herring when the season closed for navigation. My dad and Byrnes would go out on the ice and set fish nets and they made an extra living besides, for getting herring. Him (pointing at his brother), instead of walking out on the dock, he was going to walk down along side the dock, slush and stuff. The first thing I know he is up to his arm pits in the water, ice water, and I couldn't go down there because I didn't want to fall in. It was all icy. So I ran up to the signal and called my dad and Mr. Byrnes. "Clayton is in the water." They tore down there and grabbed him again.
C - Now I've got arthritis today.

Richard L. Moehl

Clayton (Foozie) Collins

What kind of signal?
C - That's where the fog horn was.

J - Where they do navigation stuff.
C - They used to call it the signal, where the fog horn was.

Did you live at Pt. Iroquois 12 months out of the year?
J - Yeah. That was our home. You know where the lighthouse is. There was a field in back. There was a 1-room school. Byrnes had three or four children.
C - He had four.
J - He had four children. They were in that school. My sister Margie and I were in that school.
C - I didn't make it. I was too young.
J - Curry had four. And then down the road, back toward the Indian settlement, where fishermen lived, Ruthiers and their children lived. Their children went to this school. It was 12 grades in one little school and I don't think it was any bigger than this room right here.

Where did the teacher live?
J - She lived with the keeper. He had a family and they had a room for her.

How was the house split up?
J - The keeper was first in the major part of the building. He had the whole left side there, the part away from the tower.
C - Yes.

Point Iroquois fog signal (left) and boat house in 1939. Notice the man at the boat house.

J - Byrnes had that, and we had the middle section. And Curry had the other section.

C - Curry was next to the tower.

J - Joe Curry was his name.

C - That whole left side was Byrnes', the keeper's.

J - So we had nine kids in that little section. Byrnes had four in the whole rest.

It was probably fun with a lot of kids round.

C - Yes, it wasn't boring.

You fished?

C - They did.

J - Where the tower is, back a little ways and down, they had a barn. It doesn't exist anymore. We had a cow. We had chickens and we had a horse. Byrnes had a horse. I don't know if he got involved with any cattle or anything. I don't think he did. I can only remember our cow was one miserable cow. She was always knocking the milk bucket over on dad. Blacky was her name, the cow.

Point Iroquois Light

Marge Beaver, Photography Plus

Come this one season, the fishing season, when they closed navigation they decided to go together and do some commercial fishing and sell their fish to make some extra money. Byrnes had a horse and we had a horse that was kept in the barn. This one winter, I would say in '27 or '28, they lost their horses through a crack in the ice. They went through in the spring time.

They were using these horses to take the nets out?
C - They had a fish shack that the horses would pull out over the hole. They would lift their nets up in the shack out of the weather.
J - They made it a dandy there. It was a good fish shack. The horses worked great.
C - It was a good fish shack until . . .
J - They were standing out there drawing in the nets. I don't know if you have ever been on the ice and the ice will crack – rrrrrrrup - right through. The horses jumped. They never stopped running until they got back by the barn. They ran around the barn and the shack hooked onto the side of the barn and they come to a stop. But, in the meantime, they had fish nets and fish scattered all the way (laugh) from the middle of the river, where they were doing their netting, up the banks. There was stuff all over the ice and the path coming up from the ice to the barn. It just scattered everything out.

Jim Collins at the interview

Your dad was OK?
J - Nobody got hurt. I don't know how they got out of the building if they were lifting nets. It might have happened when they were putting the nets out the back, out of their way. Nobody got hurt. The fish shack got wrecked.
C - No, it wasn't in too much of a good piece when . . .
J - That was an experience that everybody remarks about.

Where did they sell their fish?
J - Eckerman. Dad had an old Model T and they would put the fish in the fish boxes in the back. I think it was a truck, a pick-up truck. They put the fish in the boxes in the back of the truck and we would drive to Eckerman to deliver the

fish. I can remember, we got kind of stuck in a snow storm one time. They took and wrapped logging chains around the rear wheels to give it pulling power. They gave it too much pulling power so they could never get the truck out of low gear into high gear. The motor would stall. He had an expression. He said, " Son of a biscuit eater." (Laugh) And he would have to get out and crank. They didn't have starters in those days. The second or third time it happened I said "Son of a biscuit eater" for him. Whap across the mouth! I was not to say that.

C - There was a lot of herring. Can you imaging the amount of fish that they caught in two years? Dad was able to save enough money to buy a new Model A for $600. They were selling the herring for 1.5¢ per pound at that time.

They were lifting a whole lot of fish in their nets. Did they salt them or ice them?
C - They snowed them. You had snow to layer in the fish boxes. The trouble there was dressing the fish. You can't deliver them with innards in them. You have to clean the fish. They must have cleaned the fish out by the ice off the dock some-where. I don't remember ever watching them cleaning the fish.

Do you remember eating a lot of fish?
C - Not then I don't, but on Huron Island we ate a lot.
J - We always had smoked herring at home.
C - You must have been eating all the fish. I wasn't getting any. I don't remember getting fish.

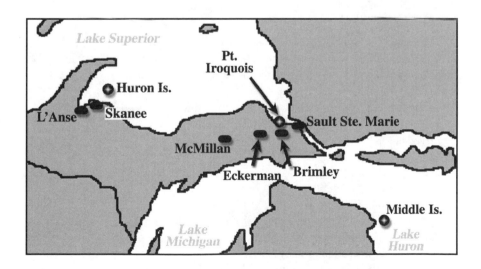

Did you have refrigeration?
J - No, there was no such thing as refrigeration in those days.

Did you cut ice?
C - I don't know.
J - I don't recall.
C - Funny they didn't, eh. Too busy fishing.

What kind of equipment was at the lighthouse? What was the light powered by?
J - We weren't allowed in the tower.
C - They couldn't have had electricity in there because I remember having kerosene lamps in the house.
J - Yes, we didn't have electricity there. They had, I forget what they call them, some kind of a lamp.
C - No electricity in the house.

What did you do for water?
C - There was a pump outside. A hand pump.

Were you in charge of water? Did you have to carry water all of the time?
C - Not me. I wasn't old enough.

That's right you were the one in the diapers.
J - They had a pump on the kitchen sink.
C - There was one in the back yard. One of those old pumps.

Do you remember taking baths?
J - No, if we took a bath it was a sponge bath in a wash tub. That's the only thing I can remember, even from Iroquois all the way through to Huron Island. We never had anything but a wash tub to do our bathing in at Skanee. In the Soo we had stuff.
C - A modern tub, running water and everything there.

You lived in town there?
C - Yes.
J - We lived at 312 Cherry St.

Did you have chores when you lived at Pt. Iroquois?
J - I don't recall. I don't remember if we went and picked the eggs from the chickens. I don't remember doing that. I only knew that if you went into that barn and the cow came around, you had better be up in the hay mow.
C - My only job there was finding fish hooks. (Laugh)

You were very good at it.
C - Excellent.
J - He wasn't the only one who did that.

There must have been recreational fishing or line fishing?
C - Not at Pt. Iroquois. No.

How about boats? Did you go out in boats there?
C - Not at Pt. Iroquois.
J - They had a boat and a boat house. I don't remember what kind of boat it was. I don't ever remember seeing them in it.

Do you remember the tender coming?
C - Not at Pt. Iroquois. Huron Islands, yes.

Do you think maybe they drove up there?
J - Oh yeah, they came. We had a road that came from Brimley.

Do you remember the inspectors coming?
J - Not at Iroquois.
C - He calls it Iroquois (ear-i-qwa) and I call it Iroquois (ear-i-koy).
J - It doesn't matter.
C - Same place.
J - There was inspection. They had to do painting, I recall. I tried to help them one time. I didn't do a good job.
C - You got fired before you got started.
J - I spilled half a gallon of red paint right over my head. I tried to take it off the shelf. I was a kid then. I was going to help them. I don't know why I got into the paint house.

Separate building?
J - The paint house, you know, was dangerous. They stored oil, kerosene, and gasoline in the paint house. They were not allowed to store those in the building.
C - They had those paint lockers in the old days. They were separate and away from the main building all of the time. They were made of brick.
J - They had a dome, a round dome on the top. They had shelves for the paint, for the gasoline, for the kerosene. They weren't allowed to carry the liquids in the houses for fire damage. You had to fill your lamps out there.

You filled the kerosene lamps out there?
J - Yes.

What was your dad's day like? Did he stand a watch?
J - Oh, yeah. Standard practice. The keeper normally picked from 8 o'clock to 12. That normally was what the keeper kept. The first assistant got from 12 to 4. The second assistant goes from 4 to 8. Each twice a day. You put in a total of eight hours. But if you were on duty, supposed to be on watch, you weren't doing maintenance, you weren't doing painting, you weren't doing anything. The other two were. They would pretty near always have anywhere from a 10- to 12-hour day. They did the maintenance, they did the painting, they did the cleaning. Then they always had to work in the signal. The signal always had to be spotless. Just like if you were in the navy. They used navy colors inside the signal. The floor was gray, navy gray. The machines were painted gray. They had a compressor. It had high wheels on it. It was a single cylinder engine. It would run, and it would get those wheels going at a pace, it had a belt on it. It would pump air, air compressor into a huge tank. Out of that tank the fog horn would blow.

This was down by the dock?
J - It was in the signal. The signal was close to the dock.

The signal is not at Pt. Iroquois any more?
J- No, it is gone. I think there might be some cribbing there. We went down there and took a look a couple of years ago. I've tried to replace my memory, where the signal was. I think you see a mound of sand and gravel off on the side as you go down the hill, before you get to the water. That would be where the signal was. The dock, the cribbing is still there. The signal was on the left hand side as you go down the hill. I can't really picture that any more.

Where did they stand the watch?
J - In the signal. The signal was where the watches were stood.

What did they do while they were on watch?
J - They had to keep timers going, the clocks, the engines. They had battery power in the signal.
C - They had generators there. They must have had a battery bank there.

What do you think they used the dock for?
C - I think they used to have a tender that brought fuel oil and stuff.
J - I don't remember a tender. Once or twice a year the tender would come.
C - They had to, or how else would they get it?

It could have come by truck?
C- Not in those days, I don't think. I doubt it.

What did you kids do all day in the summer time?
C - Play, what do you do when you are four years old?
J - Do you see those trees that are down in there?
C - There was a tire that hung from those trees down there.
J - We had a great big tree that had a big long rope tied to a tire. You'd get in that tire and you would swing across a crevice back and forth.
C - There was a gully like that you would swing across.

Between the house and the water?
Yep.
J - It had to be a gully. You didn't want to walk in that area because all of the sewer went down into that gully.

From the outhouse?
J - No, from the kitchen sink. We didn't have any inside toilets.

Did you have an outhouse?
C - Yeah. It was an outhouse.
J - I can't remember that.
C - It was right out in the back yard.
J - I don't remember it.

You don't remember how many holes?
C - It had at least two.
J - It wasn't much better than a farming family.

Did you have a garden?
J - I don't remember a garden.

Just the animals?
J - Must have been a garden of some kind.
C - Must have.
J - We had vegetables a lot.

Was there anything special you ate all of the time?
J - Wait a minute.

C - Potatoes.

J - They did have a garden, yes. Because they had it fenced in, I remember, with barb wire.

So the chickens wouldn't get in?

J - The cow. It would keep the cow from getting in the garden.

C - Keep the kids out.

J - I don't know if it was my parent's, or the others', or they all went together on a garden.

You cooked separately?

J - Oh, yeah.

C- Yes, they were like three separate apartment buildings.

What did your parents do for recreation?

C - Keep house. I don't remember.

J - Worked and had kids.

Do you remember them playing cards?

C - Nope.

Going into town?

J - We used to go to. . . They used to have a mailman walk from the Indian settlement to deliver mail. They had a post office just as you come down from Brimley. The Indian store that is right there now is about where it was. There is a lot of sand on the road between there and Iroquois Light.

Is that where you went to get groceries?

J - I think so. We did our grocery shopping in Brimley. My dad's sister and her husband and three kids lived in Brimley. My Aunt Elizabeth. My dad was the oldest one in his family. Then there was brother Bill, then after him was Aunt Elizabeth, and then there was Aunt Becky, and Uncle Arch was the youngest one in the family.

They all lived in Brimley?

J - No, my Uncle Bill went to Detroit. He's the one that got into a business of escalators and elevators.

Did you get into town very often?

J - Not too often.

C - No.

Did your dad get something like a vacation?
C - Not when you were on a land station.
J - He got the winter off.
C - He was there during the depression.
J - There was a depression in the Soo too. And we were still on depression when we moved up to Huron Island. That was in '36 the family went to Huron Island. Dad went there in '35.
C - Do you remember our first movie? (Laugh) It was at the Indian Mission there. They had a tent. They must have had electricity.
J - They had a projector.
C - It was just a tent. Somebody come there with a tent and a movie projector. He showed a movie. It cost 10 cents.

What was the movie?
C - Charlie Chaplin. Who else? It was at the Indian Mission.
J - That was part of the movies. The main movie was a Tom Mix movie.
C - That was his era, yeah. It was silent. Charlie Chaplin was silent.
J - They beat him up and threw him in a trunk and attached the trunk to a train. The train was going down the track with the trunk behind. I remember that part. I don't remember the end of the movie.

How about your first ice cream cone?
J - I don't know if we got into ice cream cones until we got to the Soo.
C - I can't remember that one. After I once had it, I never stopped.

Did you have anything like bicycles?
C - No, we didn't get a bicycle until we moved to Skanee. That was back in 1939 or 1940 we got our first bicycle.
J - I was 16 or 17.

Any of the kids of the other keepers still alive?
J - I know that Betty Byrnes is with the preservation association.
C - There is one that just died. I don't know if it was Betty or Nan. She was living in California. She just died not too long ago.
C - Both of Curry's boys got killed in the war.
J - Curry got the keeper of the lighthouse in Marquette. Dad got Huron Island. But before he got Huron Island he was at Stannard Rock for a year, and he was at Manitou, up by the Copper County. Then this opening came for keeper here (Huron Island) and he took it.

After Middle Island?
J - He was two years at Middle Island.
C - He was only there one year.
J - OK, one year.
C - Then he transferred to Stannard Rock.
J - We still lived in the Soo.

What years was he at Stannard Rock?
J - That one year.
C - Probably '33.
J - In '34 he was at Manitou. In 1935 he went to Huron Island.

From Point Iroquois he went to Stannard Rock?
C- No, he went to Middle Island first. That is down by Alpena. He went there for one year.
J - I only know it was in 1932 we moved to the Soo.
C - '31 That is where I started to kindergarten. That is why I remembered that.

You were little when you were there.
J - Yes, I was there until I was nine years old, when he went to Middle Island.

Middle Island
1931-1932?

Your dad went to Middle Island. Did you live year-round in the Soo?
C - We went to Middle Island one summer. The summer of '32. It was brick.

How was it different at Middle Island?
C - There was a Coast Guard station there right close to the lighthouse. Remember the time that we discovered . . .? My brother and I walked up in the woods one day in back of the lighthouse. We discovered some bottles of pop under a canvas hidden in the woods. So we got in there. We didn't have a way to open them. We didn't have an opener or anything so we broke the necks off. We drank it. It was pop. We later found out that dad and one of the other guys had made some pincherry wine. That's what we were drinking. We were drinking their wine. I was only six years old then.
C - We never heard anything about that either, did you?
J - No.

Middle Island today

Wayne Sapulski

Did you get drunk?
J - I got sick.
C - No. (Laugh)
J - That wine didn't taste too sweet to me. I wasn't really crazy about it.
C - We thought it was pop. Boy, this was awful pop. It isn't like what you get in the store.
J - On the upper end of the island, Middle Island, there used to be a lot of these sand cherries. We used to go there and eat those sand cherries. I did. Then there were some wild peas. Did you ever hear of wild green peas? They grow along the lake shore. They were just as sweet as could be. But they were little, tiny. Nothing like you get in the garden. I had some of them. I went over to the Coast Guard shack. He (Clayton) is puffing on a corn cob pipe. (Laugh)
C - When you hang around with older people you learn a lot of bad habits. (Laugh)
J - I had a couple of puffs. I got sick. So I left him at the Coast Guard and I went home and I laid on the davenport. Some how or other they wanted to know where you were. I said, "The last I saw him he was down at the Coast Guard shack. I don't know where he is now." Everybody turned out to find him – he was lost. Nobody knew where he was. They had the Coast Guard out looking all over the island, trying to find this kid. He couldn't have fallen in the water and drowned, you know. He's got to be on the island somewhere. Finally they found him. He had crawled in behind the davenport. He was sleeping behind the davenport. I was laying on top of the davenport, sick.

Stannard Rock
1933

You went to Middle Island only one summer. You went back to the Soo. Your dad went to Stannard Rock. Was that good news or bad news?
C - That was bad news.
J - We'd be alone.
C - That wasn't good.
J - He went from second assistant to first assistant. (Jim and Clayton discussed this and decided they didn't really know if he went from second to first assistant.)

When did he become full keeper?
C - 1935 at Huron Island.

Did you ever get out to Stannard Rock?
C, J - No.

How did he feel about it?
C - He didn't like it.
J - He said once in the fall, when the waves come and hit the building, it knocked everything out of the shelves. He said he decided that that was not going to be his station.
C - He transferred out of there as soon as an opening came at Manitou or any place.
C - Can you imagine there were two men that stayed on Stannard Rock? John Wilks from Marquette, he put in 31 seasons on Stannard Rock.

Was he a bachelor?
J - I don't know.
C - I don't know. There was another man, Sormunen, he put in 27 seasons there. Can you imagine? On Stannard Rock. How did those two guys get along all those years? They never transferred out. Evidently they liked it. You've got to be a special kind of a person to be like that. How many games of cribbage did they play, I wonder? Wow.

Maybe they never saw each other if they were standing opposite watches?
C - I don't know.
C - They must have eaten a lot of fish.

Did they catch fish out there?
C - Oh, that's one of the best fishing places in Lake Superior for lake trout.

Did your dad fish out there?
C - He never talked about it.

Huron Island
1935-1952

He applied to transfer out to Huron Island?
C - No, he went to Manitou Island from there.
J - One season there. We were still in the Soo. We moved up here to Skanee in 1935, after school was out. At that time we had an old Model A. It is impossible for a family to move with a Model A if you've got five kids. My brother and I were taken to my grandma's place in McMillan. We spent the summer there, well, most of the summer.
C - In 1935 my dad didn't bring us along because they didn't have enough beds.

Did they buy a house in Skanee?
C - No they rented one. There weren't enough beds on Huron Island for me and Jim so we had to stay with my grandma in McMillan in '35.

Were the beds you were using your own beds or the government beds?
C - They were our own beds.
J - You had to furnish your own.
C - The government didn't supply anything but a stove for you. That's about all.

Was the assistant keeper's building there when you got there?
C - Yes, it was there but dad and Campbell worked, they helped finish that building in 1935 I think. They helped finish it off so it could be lived in.

At Huron Island your dad was the keeper? Then John Campbell?
C - He was first assistant.

Was there somebody else there?
C - Martin Peterson.
J - He retired from Huron Island. His home was in Baraga.

The gathering rock behind Huron Island Light. This photo was taken before the generators were added to the right side of the lean-to. Notice that there is no chimney and no door.

He's not still alive?
J - No, he was old then.
C - He passed away a long time ago.
J - He was a nice old gentleman. He always wore his lighthouse cap when he was on duty. He had one of those old-fashioned cigarette holders.
C - Like President Roosevelt had.
J - That was one of his hallmarks.

When did your dad wear his uniform?
J - I think the only time he wore his uniform was when he come ashore. He had to dress to come ashore, drive the boat. Also, he wore it out at the island if we were going to have an inspection, naturally. They knew ahead of time when the *Amaranth* was going to come around with the inspector. Then we had to have everything cleaned and polished.

J - They were expecting the inspector and had just gotten through painting the top of the tower. Nice, finished black paint. The flag was flying up there nice. We were given the duty of sitting out in front of the lighthouse with a 22 to keep the seagulls from landing up on top of the tower. We were picking off the sea gulls. We would hit them and watch them and they would flop and then they would go over and pretty soon nose dive way down to the lake. I don't remember how many we shot, but at least we kept them away from messing up the top of the lighthouse tower.

That was one of your chores?
J - Yeah. We enjoyed that. That was a good job.
C - We had chores out there. Hauling water.
J - Never ended. You didn't go anywhere without a bucket. If you went to the signal, the dock, it don't matter. The young kids had a little 2-quart bucket, coffee can. They had to carry the coffee can. We got a little bit older, we got a little bit bigger bucket. When we got older yet we got the 12-quart bucket. Two of them.

I showed the row boat picture.
C - There it is.
J - That's the best rowboat I ever rowed. You would never find another one like it. That thing would just shhhh . . .
C - We used to make that go so fast that we couldn't keep up with the oars.
C - That's where we learned how to fish, how to troll for lake trout with that boat.
J - Two sets of oars in that boat. It would just fly.

C - He and I would get a pair of oars in there and we would get going and we'd get that boat going so fast we couldn't keep up with it with the oars.

J - I never ever rowed a boat like that before. And control, you could stand up on the edge and the boat would not flip over. That boat was cedar stripped. That is the best kind of boat you could build.

C - It was an old-timer. You know what they went and did with it? They burned it.

J - Idiots!

C - Too old. They didn't want it in the service any more.

And they wouldn't let you have it?
C - Nope.

Was it painted or natural?
C - Painted.
J - Gray, navy gray.

Looking at the Huron Island motor boat.
C - There's the old boat.

J - Oh, my goodness. Oh, that one. I was thinking of the one, the first trip we went out to island in. That was the old one-lunger, it was an open boat. It had a canvas up front with what was supposed to be cellophane to look through for driving the boat.

C - It was nothing but a spray shield is all it was.

J - Yah, and we hit some waves. I forget if it was you or me that had our back to that and we got socked in the back with water. I don't ever remember being sea sick though. Never ever.

C - Did Dick happen to tell you about the time we had the band, the WPA band out there?

No.

C - This one time John Campbell went ashore. The boat used to go in at least once a week for provisions, mail, or whatever. This one time John had to go to town to get something for the station, for one of the motors or something. At that time he met Chief Welsh, a big Indian, a Soux Indian from the Dakotas. He was the leader of the band, the county band, at that time. He talked Chief into bringing the band out there to the island and give us a little program. So we had to go into the mouth of the Huron River on that Sunday. The weather was nice. Nice day and everything. My dad and I made the first trip. We went in with the motor launch and we pulled that row boat there behind to put the instruments in, you know. There was about 13 guys, and that little boat would only carry about six. So we had to make two trips. They come out there with all their instruments and got up to the lighthouse. Right there between the two houses is that big flat rock that you see there. It is like a stage. They got up there and they started playing. At that time there were hundreds of sea gulls living on the island due to the presence of all the commercial fishermen in the area. And that was their home. Well, I'm telling you, the seagulls had never heard anything like a band. They were used to the fog horn and boat motors and the wind and whatever, but not a band. In no time at all there were hundreds of them, they came. It was blitzkrieg. They sky was full of them. The band was playing and the seagulls were squawking. Such a racket. And then, pretty soon, the gulls started leaving their droppings. Oh, my. Well everybody was just running for shelter. The band, they kept on playing. They wanted to finish their song. They were getting dirtied on, and their instruments, and every thing. It was so comical. I ran for cover. I hid up along side of the stone house. Other people they just ran in the houses and everything. They took off. After a while the band quit playing. Then the sea gulls kind of settled down. Then they started to play again and the sea gulls came back again. They came from miles. The main colony was over two miles away. They heard that noise. They had to come and find out what was making all that noise. The sky was just full of them.

Jim Collins and John Campbell, notice the band members standing in the background

Campbell family photo

Well, anyway, they finally settled down and realized that the band wasn't going to hurt them. The band finished their program. Then they had a picnic and we had to take them back to the mouth of the river again. Dick decided to ride in that skiff on the way back on the last trip. His dad was running the boat and pulling the skiff. All of a sudden his dad looked back and Dick wasn't even there. The boat, everything was gone. Dick was way back. The rope had come untied, or broke, or something. Dick was left floating alone out there. He had a pair of oars, I guess. He was rowing for the island with the oars. His dad had to go back and pick him up. That was really comical. Those sea gulls, I never saw anything like that in my life.

Was there other music out there?
C - Radio, yes.
J - Dad always listened to the Detroit Tiger baseball games.

You could get the Detroit Tigers out there?
J - We could catch a station from Houghton.
C - WHDF, how could you forget that? They had the Corn Cobbers (music group) every Saturday afternoon..
J - Getting back to the sea gulls. The Huron Islands are a group of several islands. The main island is where the lighthouse is. The next main island is called several names, it was known as East Island, Nelson Island, or MacIntyre Island. On the other end of that island is a place, a sea gull rookery, called Gull Island

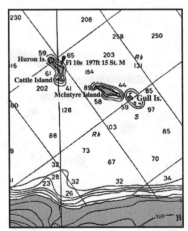

C - That is a couple of miles. Those sea gulls were flying clear over here.
J- MacIntyre, he was a commercial fisherman there. The original name for that island was East Island. Then the other was Sea Gull Island, yeah Gull Island.

Notice how deep the water is around these islands.
Apparently Cattle Island was named for the cattle marooned on the island from a ship wreck.

Dick was talking about Cattle Island. Which one is that?
J - That is right close to the boat house. There is a passage between the main island and Cattle Island. It is about 40 or 50 feet apart. You can drive through with a boat.

It is deep enough?
Yes.

Did you guys play instruments? Was there any music you made?
J - Not me.
C - Not out there.

This was your first experience with a musical band?
J - I never heard a band before. In the Soo we went to 4th of July parades. My dad's youngest brother was in Fort Brady, he was a "d" "i", drill instructor.

At the Soo?
J - Yes, this was back in the same years we were there. He was in Fort Brady when we were living in Iroquois Light. When we moved to the Soo, dad and mom rented a house. Then we rented two or three rooms to my dad's brother and his wife and nephew that was born there, Dick Collins. His real name is Lawrence. My dad's youngest brother's name is Lawrence. (too) They didn't want to get them mixed up so he got the nickname of Dick.
C - Remember that storm that fall we went out to the island? Dad took us out there fishing. You wouldn't believe.
J - You would have to be there to witness it.
C - You've seen pictures of how far the lighthouse is up from the water. OK, that night an awful storm came up. There was lightning, rain and wind.
J - Huge wind.
C - Our bedroom window was right in the front of that stone house.
J - At the base of the lighthouse tower.
C - We lived in the stone house at that time. Our bedroom window was right to the left of the tower. It was a north wind that night. It must have picked up to 45 – 50 mph. The rain was coming against our bedroom window. Big waves were hitting the front of the island. The wind would pick the wave up and throw it against our bedroom window.
J - It sounded like it was going to smash in the whole wall. It thundered.
C - I was 11 years old.

How far above the water level do you think the house was?
C - I know that the top of the tower from the water is 192 feet. So I would say maybe 172 feet and it is back quite a ways. The waves were coming against our bedroom window. It was in October.

When would you come off the island?
J - School.

Campbell family photo

Huron Island Lighthouse sits on the rock about 172 feet above the water level.

C - The family would come off maybe a week before school would start. Maybe the first of September.

You stayed in Skanee?
C - Yes.
J - We rented there.
C - There was a school there.

Did you play with the Campbells?
C - Oh, we played with Dick all the time.
J - Him and his sister..
C - We went swimming. We used to build rafts. Go fishing together.
J - We tried to fish.
C - We used to build a lot of rafts. Me and Dick, we had kind of a competition going. Any time we would get some kind of a wind, say from the west or south, we would run down by the boat house and start searching the shoreline for net floats. We would get those aluminum net floats. We'd get maybe three cents for them from the commercial fishermen in Skanee where we docked the boat. They'd get torn loose from the nets and the wind would bring them in. But we were always building rafts or swimming together, catching minnows around the dock or something. Something to do all of the time. We made our own fun really. Dick and I liked fishing. We even used to get little hunks of net from the commercial fishermen, pieces that they would take out of their nets and throw away. When the lighthouse boat would land at their dock in Skanee, boy, we would make a bee line for their junk pile and see if there was anything there. We would get a little piece of net and we'd go out on our raft and set it in and we'd catch a sucker, or a herring once in a while. We were having a good time. This one time we decided we were going have our own net winder and our own shack and everything. They had a mortar box that they used for mixing mortar. Dick and I took that mortar box and that was the base of our new shack. Where we got all the boards from, I don't know. But we built a little shack. We even had a little table in there, a window or two. Then we put a net winder outside to put our nets on. We had a good time.

Did you catch any fish though?
C - Once in a while we would catch a fish. Not too often.

If you caught a fish, would you eat it?
C - Oh, yeah. You bet! There was another shack on a little island not too far from the boat house. We used to go over and play in it. It was nothing but a little old shack. There might be a picture of that.

Campbell family photo

Dick Campbell with the shed made out of a mortar box, notice the fish net winder on the far side of the shed

J - It was right between the main island and Cattle Island. It was just an outcropping of rocks sitting there. Somebody put a shack there. It was a place to go if you wanted to get away from everybody. You could go sit in that shack.

How did you get over there?
J - Swim.
C - We'd swim or take the raft. Once in while we would swipe the rowboat. We weren't allowed to use that too much. Dad wanted to make sure it was kept in good shape. There are no sand beaches out there. It is all rock.

In the picture it looks like that boat is sitting on some kind of ramp.
J - Yes, it is a ramp. I used to go with that little boat down by the signal. I had homemade trawling spoons that dad made. Dad used to smoke Prince Albert. He formed a trolling spoon out of a tin can with tin snips. Then he would solder in a steel line and a hook on the end. I tied on to the loop for hooking on my fishing line, a plain white cotton line. I would troll for lake trout. I caught lake trout on homemade spoons. Matter of fact, I got one steelhead. I thought I had the bottom. I was backing up with the oars. All of a sudden a fish jumped along side of the

boat. So I had to hurry up and row. I didn't want to lose it. I hauled it aboard. It was something like a 12 or 13 pound steelhead on a homemade fishing spoon.

C - It was a very unique life. When you're born into it you don't realize how unique it was. Huckleberry Finn and Tom Sawyer didn't have anything on us at all.

Did you ever get hurt?
J - Oh, yeah, lots of times. Step on a nail.

Broken bones or something like that?
J - No.
C - That kind of a life. . . When I think back, it taught us so much. Nature. Patience. To sacrifice. To be careful. You didn't want to be stubbing your toe and falling on your knees. There was nothing but rock out there. You don't land on anything soft. It taught you so much.

What kind of shoes did you have?
J - Tennis shoes.
C - Those good old 50¢ tennis shoes. You wore them until your foot came out the sides. What a life!

What was your dad's life like now that he was keeper?
J - They were busy. They hardly had time for anything but work. They were always painting. They were always cleaning. If a motor broke down they had to tear the motor apart and rebuild it. In other words you had to be a master mechanic, a good man with a paint brush, and you had to know how to clean up. You had to polish. You had to know how to polish brass. You just did not have any time off.

What kind of chores did your mom do?
J - Cooking and washing.
C - That was a big chore for a woman with five kids and no running water. No refrigerator when we first went out there.

How did she do the washing?
J - There was a cistern. They had rain troughs on the building that went down into the cistern below the kitchen. A big tank. You had a hand pump to pump that. But you didn't want to use that water for anything but washing clothes. As far as washing, you had a hand plunger.

C - Don't forget the scrub board.

J - When mom got busy it was either me or him, or Marilyn or Laurel, that had to stand there with that plunger and plunge by hand to do the washing. People don't know how good it is to have a washing machine.

C - Hand ringer.

Did you hang your clothes out on a line?

C - Yep. The government didn't buy that either. You had to buy your own clothes line.

How often do you think your mom did that?

C - Probably once a week providing there was water in the cistern. Otherwise, you had to wait until it rained to get enough water in there. It is a long ways to haul water from the lake, a half mile by pail. All up hill.

She never took the clothes down to the lake?

C - I think she did once. We had to go to the lake because there wasn't enough water. With five kids, clothes don't stay clean very long. I've got to tell you the story about the smoke house. When we first got out there we just took off. We were going to explore and find out what kind of a place this was. I don't know who discovered it, him or my older sister, Marjorie. This stinky, little, old shack that was hidden off the trial down in the brush. I don't know who got the idea, him and Marjorie probably, they were the oldest ones. I didn't have a brain yet. They went and got some hammers and we tore that little, stinky, old shack apart, board by board. We couldn't imagine why anybody would want anything like that, it stunk so bad. We hauled it off to another part of the island and we were going to build a shack of our own out of it. We got that all completed, almost. Then we heard ma calling, "Supper kids." We went up there she took a look at us and she said, "What in the world have you kids been doing?" We were just dirty, and black, and stinky, and everything. Well, we come to find out we had torn down the smoke house. The keeper's smoke house! That's the smoke house they had been using to smoke lake trout for I don't know how many years. It was there when dad got there. They built a new one down by the fog signal so they could keep their eye on it. (Laugh) Yep, that was something else. We tore down the smoke house.

J - Part of that smoke house ended up on that one raft. We built a raft and we had a shack on it. We had a hole in the middle, remember that?

C - Oh, yeah.

J - You could look down there.

C - You should have seen that raft.

J - Two poles, they were about that big around and at least 20 feet long. I don't know how in the world they got up there on the Huron Islands. They got washed up on the shore. We made a point on it, like a boat. We put the shack on there. We'd go pushing that thing around with a paddle. One time we were darn near out to the end of Cattle Island and the old man, father, came down to the dock, and we really caught it. We were too far from shore. If the wind came along it would not be a good deal. We really caught the dickens for that, "You guys don't go beyond that rock." But we had it tied up alongside the dock. It was a neat little thing. We used to use it to set nets.

How did you get along with the mainland kids?
C - OK. We hardly saw them all summer.
J - During the beginning, when we first moved there, you were a stranger. You are coming into an area where everybody is established. You're unknown. You are off color. I don't know how you would explain it. It took a little while before we got acquainted enough so that we didn't get into too many fights.

Did you have nicknames?
C - When we lived in the Soo, someone started calling me blackie because I hated to wash up, I guess. I carried that for a while until we moved out of the Soo and then I lost that name. Then I acquired a new one, a friend of mine started calling me Foozie. That stuck ever since 1941.

How did that come about?
C - From eating peaches. Back in 1941 we started coming to school in L'Anse. When we lived in Skanee we had to walk a mile to catch a bus, winter and summer. Then we had to ride about 25 miles to get to school in L'Anse. It was a long day. At that time the grade school in Skanee was getting "commodities," they used to call it, not welfare but . . .
C - They had a hot lunch program going in Skanee for the grade school kids. Our bus driver would pick up the commodities in L'Anse and haul them out there. Well, it just so happened this one time I was awfully hungry. The bus driver, he didn't like me, so he made me sit in the back of the bus where he could watch me in that big mirror. He put me right by those peaches and I just couldn't resist. I took a couple of those peaches out of there and put them in my lunch bucket. He caught me doing it. He kicked me off the bus right at the Skanee main intersection. He kicked me off the bus. I was mad. I wouldn't let him get by me. I stayed right in front of the bus. He was ready to kill me. I was kicked off the bus for three days. I wasn't allowed to ride on his bus any more. It was his bus, not the school's. He leased it to the school. Well, the news got around school and one of my friends

started calling me peach fuzz. Then he shortened it to fuzzy. Then, for some reason or another, he started calling me foozie. That name has hung on me since 1941. Even my doctor didn't know my real name. (Laugh)

Dick was talking about when they came to town, the first thing they did was get an ice cream cone.
J - That had to be in L'Anse.
C - There was no ice cream in Skanee.
J - They had cold soda at the Rhinelander's store. That building is still there.

In Skanee?
Yes

But not groceries?
J - Now nobody is in it at all. It ended up as a co-op store through the 40s. When I came home from the service, Rhinelander had sold the store to the co-op. It was one of those co-op stores that was dealing in about everything, feed for cattle. The guys who worked in the store had to do butchering. They had to wait on the counters.

Back to the lighthouse, do you remember your dad having more paperwork?
C - Oh yeah, there was always a lot of stuff to do there. They had to keep track of everything.
J - When they were on duty they had a log book to work on. Each guy had to log in. They had to keep that log about when they came in and when they left. They had to account for every hour. They didn't have a wind thing, but they had to record the wind direction approximately. The clouds, if it was moonlight or cloudy, or if it was raining. Whatever was going on was put in the log book.

Where did he write in the log book?
J - At the signal, way up on the west end of the island, northwest.

How far from the house was the signal?
C - It was a good half mile.

How long would it take you to walk down there?
C - 15 to 20 minutes if you ran.

On the other end of the island was the boathouse, right?
C - We were entertained there for two summers, remember? The Coleman dredge came in 1937-38 maybe '39. They were building that breakwater in Marquette. A big scow came out there that had a big clamshell bucket. They were picking up all these big boulders out around the island. They would load that up and they had a tug, the Coleman tug, that would pull it to Marquette. Then they would come back and get another load. We were entertained with them. We would sit on the shore and watch them by the hour. They had some big boulders they were taking off the island and then out of the water also.

Did they come ashore ever?
C - No. I remember once in a while that guy operating that big clam, he would get a big boulder up, and he would come over by us and drop it and splash us and get us all wet. And every once in a while they would feel sorry for us and throw us an orange or something.

What were the rules? You couldn't boat out past a certain rock?
J - With that raft. If you were in the rowboat, that was different.

Campbell family photo

Huron Island rocks. The flecks in the sky are sea gulls.

C - We didn't go too far with the raft. Remember the old gas tanks that were in the little shack on that little island? They had some gas tanks out of an old boat that they kept over there, I don't know why. They didn't throw anything away.

J - It must have been a 40- or 50-gallon tank.

C - Maybe 40. They were not quite triangle shaped. One end was square. They were flat and about that deep.

J - Flat in the back and on an angle.

C - We decided to make little boats out of them. So we got a cold chisel and hammer and cut a chunk right out, and sat in there and rowed it like a little canoe.

How were they for riding?

C - They were pretty tippy (Laugh)

J - Tricky (Laugh).

C - Dick has that picture of us. There was me, a couple of my sisters and one of his sisters sitting on them. We got so that we could sit on it. We cut one hole out of one end to sit in it. If you were just trying to ride on them they were really tippy. A lot of time you would fall off. We had little boards that we would paddle around with. There was so much to learn out there, unreal.

Richard L. Moehl

Boat house on south side of Huron Island

Did your dad ever let you into the lantern room there?
J - No, we were not allowed to go up.
C - Once in a while we were allowed to go up if he was with us. Otherwise, no.
J - We were on the first floor and that was it. We had to go in and out the front door or out through the kitchen. If you go out the front door, you had a board walk out front that you could walk around the side to the kitchen. You could go in and out of that front door to the tower. Our bedrooms were on the side, and you walked in a little bit further and you came into the living room.

Did the Campbell kids ever live in the house that you can remember?
C - They lived in that white house. They had a bedroom or two upstairs in the stone house.

Were there three floors in this house?
C - Two, Martin and Maude had a bedroom upstairs in the stone house too, at the same time. There was one big room upstairs. That was Martin and Maude's bedroom. They had a kitchen in back of the white house. The Campbells had the front part of the white house with one bedroom in there with a kitchen and a living room, two closets upstairs of the stone house that they used for bedrooms.

Did the second floor also go into the tower?
C - Yes.

Was it a spiral staircase?
C - Oh, yeah. Boy, I hated those things. Coming down especially. There was nothing to hang on to. There isn't much to step on, one little stumble and you are gone.

Did your dad ever complain about that?
No.

Do you remember ever hearing about any problems that they had with the light or fog horn?
J - The generator broke down.
C - They had problems all of the time, something broken down. That one time, remember when the boat sank? When we first went out there in 1936 they had an old boat, it was an open boat with no cabin on. It was an old double ender, they

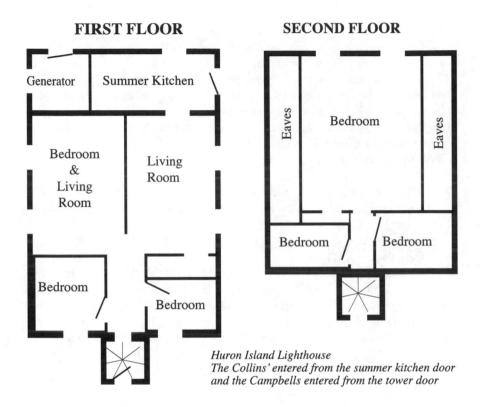

FIRST FLOOR   **SECOND FLOOR**

Huron Island Lighthouse
The Collins' entered from the summer kitchen door
and the Campbells entered from the tower door

called it. Like a surf boat with just a canvas spray shield on it. It had an old motor in it that you had to crank like an old Model T. It was one cylinder.

J - Thumk, thumk, thumk, thumk . . .

C - Every once in a while they had to go someplace with it. This one time they went ashore with it and they came back and they were going to do something the next day. So, instead of pulling the boat up into the boat house, which they usually did, they left it tied up to the dock so they wouldn't have to go through all that. That night a storm came up out of the west and came in and the waves hit the dock and over the dock into the boat. They had the boat on the inside of the dock where they thought it was safe. It wasn't safe. The waves filled that boat right up with water and sank it. It was tied up. It was hanging there from the rope, full of water. They had quite a job of bailing that all out.

J - Getting the engine started again. Getting that all dried off.

C - They never did that again with that old boat.

J - Nope.

What pulled the boat up into the boat house?
C - They had a tramway with a big hand winch.
J - It was like a railroad car with small wheels. It had a cradle on it. You would drive your boat onto the cradle. You tied it off onto the tram and then you had a cable. You had a 2-man thing, one guy on one handle and one guy on the other.

Did they use you?
C - Yes, we used to do it. That is how you pulled the car.
J - It had a click on it, every notch it would go over. So if you wanted to stop and rest, you could stop and that would hold. As you rolled it up it kept clicking over the gears.
C - It stayed on a slant all the time. It never leveled off.

Where did you spend most of your time?
C - At the dock. We were swimming, catching minnows. Dick and I used to make little toy boats. We would put a string on them and a stick and walk around the dock and pull them around. We were hard on their 2X4s. It is hard to get lumber out there. You've got to go all the way to L'Anse or Skanee to get it. We used to cut off a piece of 2X4 and make a little boat out of it. And nails, oh my gosh. We must have used up half a keg of nails out there that one summer. Building boats, rafts and the shack. Funny we didn't catch a lot of dickens for stealing their mortar box that time.
J - I wasn't involved in that one.
C - No, Dick and I did that. They used to call us the two Finlanders because we were always fishing. Or making believe we were fishing. Remember when we found that old row boat in Skanee?
J - Yeah, we hauled that out.
C - We found an old boat on the shore in Skanee one time. Dad pulled it out to the island for us. Dick and I just wanted to have nets and everything. We would find fishermen's old net buoys that would break loose and wash up on the shore. We would do anything, we took wire and everything else, to put that darn buoy out there to make it look like we had a net there. We'd make believe we would go out and lift our nets. Pull up all that wire and everything into the boat. I don't even know where all that wire came from. We scavenged around. We had a lot of fun just making believe.

I think Dick told of one time when one of you went with him and actually pulled up somebody's net.
J - We did. We almost got in trouble with that one. We got discovered.
C - Dad and Mr. Campbell didn't want us kids monkeying around like that. You know kids, they have to learn.
J - I was trolling my rowboat and I snagged onto a net. They put the net too close to the island, it was their fault. (Laugh) Where I was fishing we got a hold of that net. "Hey, let's see if there are any fish." So you start that net, hauling and hauling. Now you are going to put the net back and it's all tangled up. "That's all right, throw it overboard, let it go." I did lose a set of hooks in it. Lucky I did that. The fisherman he came up to the house, "Did you guys do any trolling out there?" "Oh, yeah, I did troll out there." "Did you happen to snag my net?" "Yes, you set it too close to the island. That is where we fish." " The next time you do that would you kindly just cut the line. I will gladly bring that trolling spoon back." Because his net was all balled up. That's better than stealing groceries.

What did your parents do for recreation?
J - They had all they could do to take care of kids. What's recreation? Sometimes a guy would come down to the signal early for his duty and they would sit down and play a game of cribbage. They had to communicate too. They would maybe be down there half hour early, they would play one or two hands of cribbage. You never left the signal or boathouse with an empty bucket. You came up with a bucket of water. Always. The men naturally could carry two buckets with no problem. Or we thought it was no problem. So we joined them.

Where did you put the water?
C - We took it into the house and put it in a big pail. That was used for cooking.

The cistern was at the house. Could the Campbells use the cistern water?
J - Yes, if there was water there.
C- It was just like a well. When they built the house they had dug a big hole in that rock and put a cistern in there. A huge tank.

Do you remember any of the maintenance crews?
C - I remember one guy that used to come. His name was Beisel. We used to call him bicycle. He used to come out there and work on . . . . I don't know if he was some kind of a specialist on machinery or the clocks, or something, I can't remember just what it was. There were different service people that had to come out there to work on things that dad and Campbell weren't that experienced on.

Where did you go from Huron Island?
J - I went to the army.
C - Dad transferred to Upper Portage Entry.
J - Dad put 17 years at Huron Island.

When did he leave?
J - In '52. He went to Upper Entry on the other side of Houghton, Calumet. That is where he retired from. It was all under Coast Guard at that time.

Did your Dad transfer from the Lighthouse Service to the Coast Guard in '39?
J - Yes, not in '39. He didn't get in until I went to the army in December '42. He was in the Coast Guard in '42. He was eligible to transfer.
C - After the war he went back into the Lighthouse Service. He got out of the Coast Guard.
J - He was in Coast Guard reserve then.
C - He got out of the Coast Guard because with family he didn't want to be transferred.
J- In 1962 he retired.

He must have loved Huron Island.
C - Yeah, but you know, when you stop and think about it, in his later years like in December, November they had to walk from that house down to the fog signal

Portage Lake Canal near Houghton, Mich.

Terry Pepper Collection

twice a day, in storms, blizzards. And that stone house was cold because there was nothing but a kerosene space heater in there. They usually got off the island about a week before Christmas. Stone is not warm and no insulation.

I imagine walking across the rocks it would get treacherous.
C - Those trails . . .

What year was he born?
1896, June 13th.

By 1952 he is 56 years old.
C - Look at us. He is 80 and I am 77.

Your dad's birthday was while you were out there. Do you remember holidays?
J - 4th of July? I don't remember anybody celebrating anything.
C - Every day was the same.
J - Maybe 4th of July, if it fell on the weekend when the boat went ashore. I don't ever remember, after we left the Soo, I don't remember seeing any celebrations, parades or anything. Even in Skanee.

How about other visitors who would come out?
J - Oh, yeah, We had a lot of that.

People coming out in their own boat?
J - We had that too. These fishermen that he was talking about, Falk. They had a 36-foot fish tug that was pointed at both ends, with full cabin. On Saturday they would completely scrub and clean that boat on the inside. Then they were hired by different groups that would come out. Ten to 15 people could come out to Huron Island to visit the island. That was a pretty regular thing on Sunday.
C - Two dollars a head.
J - The Falks furnished them with food, picnics. They had beer on board. They would go and even lift nets and give those people some fish to take home with them. Almost every Sunday, not everyone. You would always look forward to Sunday because you would get to see somebody different.

They would park their boat at the boat house?
J - Yeah, or they could park at the signal, too. But you can't anymore. There used to be a dock at both ends. The one at the signal is demolished. It is gone.
C - They blew it up.

Did you go into town on a regular day, like always on Saturday?
C - There wasn't room for everybody. You had to take your turn.
J - John Campbell or dad would pilot the boat. I don't remember Martin, he was too old. I thought he was old. He looked old.

Campbells left before your dad left?
J - Oh, yeah.

Who replaced them?
J - Coast Guard.
C - They were mostly younger Coast Guard. My dad was quite disappointed about that because they didn't take care of the place. I took my dad back to Huron Island one summer, I think it was in 1954, a couple years after he had left. When he got out there and saw the shape the quarters were kept. . . They had young Coast Guards with their wives. They weren't doing anything. The floor in the main building was dirty, they hadn't scrubbed it for weeks. He said, "Clayton, get me out of here!"

Have you been back?
C - I never tire of going back there.
J - We have been there a lot of times.
C - I enjoy every time.
J - We always walk the island.

What were the floors like?
C- Hard wood, painted. They had linoleum on them.

Were there tin ceilings in that lighthouse?
C - No, plaster.

Was the woodwork painted?
C - Oh yeah. They kept everything painted.

Do you remember the colors in the house?
C - White and gray. No decorations.

Woodwork was painted, not varnished?
C - All paint. That navy gray.

What was the furniture like?
C - Very simple, and plain, wood.

Something bought or something made?
C - Some of it was made. I remember a little night stand we had by our bunk that was made out of balsam poles and an orange crate.

Did the Peterson's leave while you were there?
J - Yes, I don't remember the year he left. We were in Skanee
C - He was there in the early '40s. He retired from there.
J - He went to his home in Baraga.

What would be a regular meal, breakfast, lunch, dinner?
C - Cold cereal or oatmeal for breakfast. Supper was the main meal. For lunch you would get a peanut butter sandwich or something. The first few years we were out there, there was no refrigeration.
J - You like canned milk? Mixed with water for your breakfast cereal, that is what you had. There was no bottled milk.
C - For supper when we first got out there, there was no refrigeration, it was mostly fish if you had fish, or salt pork. Because there was no way to keep meat.
J - My mother was always canning. There wasn't a season that went by when we were on shore that we didn't pick berries. Whatever berry season there was, everybody was picking berries. I hated berry picking ever since. You spent your day on shore picking strawberries. Or we've got to go out here and pick some raspberries. That's the worse berry there is to pick, I thought.
C - I thought it was fun because it got us away from cutting wood. It was a lot easier than cutting wood.

You cut wood too?
C - Oh, yeah on shore. With a hand saw.

When you went to shore?
J - She did all of the canning. She canned everything you could think of.

Then she carried that back out to the island?
J -Yes, we did take out canned goods.

Did she can meat?
C - One time I guess somebody shot a deer illegally and she canned some of that.

Were there any deer to shoot on the island?
J - Rabbits.
C - There were rabbits out there.
C - We used to catch little rabbits out there, by hand. We'd see them on the trail many times. They would run and go into a little hole under a rock. We'd reach in there and pull them out. Remember Marilyn took one up to the house that one time? A little bunny like that, and put it in the kitchen. Well the poor little thing, it was doing its business all over the rug. It would try to run on that linoleum and it was slipping and sliding all over. Mother said, " Get that out of here. Look it is messing." It was piddling here and piddling there. Poor little rabbit. We finally let it go. There was, there probably still is, a wood tick out there. They are real small. They would get on these rabbits and suck them dry.
J - Kill them. Their ears would fill up with them.
C - We would catch these rabbits and pull these ticks off.

Would they get on you?
J - I never got one.
C - I felt so sorry for them but what could you do?

How about the time the bobcat was caught?
C - That thing was out there for two years that we knew of.
J - It killed all of the rabbits.
C - It ate a lot of rabbits.

How did they catch the bobcat?
J - In a trap. John Campbell caught it.
C - That island was thick with what they called ground hemlock. It was thick.
J - You couldn't walk through it.
C - Rabbits could hardly get through it. There were lots of rabbits out there.

Did you eat rabbit?
J - No, not in the summer.
C - They would eat some in the fall.
J - They had the 22 out there to kill a rabbit for fresh meat.
C - In the fall they were isolated out there for at least a month. They lived a lot on dried beans and peas and salt pork, rice and stuff like that.

No tenders got out there?
C - No, they were not able to catch fish. They put the boat away for the winter when the ice would start forming. There was no way to get ashore.

How did the tender pick them up?
C - The tender was able to get them off the island.
J - By the signal.
C - Sometimes they couldn't. They would have to wait for the weather to calm down.

Where would the tender take them?
J - Up to Houghton.
C - Houghton or Marquette.

What do you remember about this spot? Flat stone on back of house.
C - That was it. Picnics there.
J - There used to be a kind of a bench out there. In the evenings if we had a really nice evening mother and dad would come out. But not dad after 8 o'clock because he would be on duty. And Mrs. Campbell and John Campbell and the kids some time. We would just gather out there and look at the sunsets. Watch the sky.
C - It was so refreshing in the evening.

Were bugs ever a problem on this island?
C - Flies (Laugh)
J - I'll tell you what.
C - The Huron River is over there about 3-1/2 or 4 miles. It is all sand in that area and every July these, they called them fish flies or sand flies, would hatch. Any time that you got a little south wind they all ended up on Huron Island. Oh, my word.

Did they bite?
C - Bite! It took me five years to gain two pounds out there! (Laugh) I never saw such. They would get so hungry. When there was a south wind, the lee side of that little white house was black with them.
J - Black.
C - If you went out of the house and wanted to go down to the fog signal or boathouse you would blouse up your pants. You tied them down with rope or string or whatever. You put a jacket over your head and, when you went out of the door, mother was there with a dish towel keeping the flies out. When you got outside you ran like "h". They would eat you alive.
J - Yeah.

Were there black flies and mosquitoes?
C - There were some mosquitoes but they didn't hardly bother you. The flies were terrible.

J - They were the ones that would demolish you. If you got out on the boat, away from the island a little bit, they would still hang on the boat If you wanted to row you had gloves and a jacket. It would be warm and you were going to sweat, naturally. But then we had what you called a rag bag in the signal. You had to go in the rag bag and drag out any kind of rag you could find to wrap around your feet. Even if you had tennis shoes those flies would get right down in there.

Big flies?
J - No, not too big. About the size of a house fly.

Did you have screens on the house?
J - Oh yeah, you had to. The house would fill up with flies some how or other. Everybody would get a towel and stand at that end of the room away from the door to the kitchen. You'd start waving your towels and work toward the door to chase all the flies out into the kitchen. You'd get them all in the kitchen and somebody would stand out there and open the door and then you had to chase all the flies out of the kitchen to the outside. One person had to stand in the doorway and keep them from coming back into the living room.
C - If you really wanted to draw them just fry some fish. Oh, they would come by the thousands. They loved fried fish. They never got it, but they liked the smell.

Was that what you ate most, fish?
C - Oh, yeah.
J - A lot of fish.
C - I'm still eating fish. Oh, I love fish.

Looking at the picture of the back of the ligthhouse.
J -That's the kitchen.
C - That's where our kitchen was here. And over here was where they kept two generators, two LeRoy generators. They were diesel. There was a battery bank in there that they charged. I think there was something like 30 some 6-volt batteries in there. That's what ran the electricity and lights and everything.

You didn't have kerosene lamps here?
C - Not there.

You had electric lights.
J - Yeah.

Looking at the upstairs of the lighthouse
C - Peterson's bedroom was up there. In the front part were the two closets that the Campbells had for bedrooms.

These walls didn't have insulation I guess.
J - No, no.

Just lath and plaster?
J - That's all.

This was your dog? His name was?
C - Skipper.

Did Skipper come with you to the island?
J - Oh, yeah. He would hit the boat and go right up into the bow of the boat and stay there until they got out.

He'd be the first?
J - No, he'd be the last.
C - He didn't like boat riding.
J - He liked to swim in the water. He liked water, but he didn't like the boat. He got sick. He'd lay up there. When we would get to the island, phew, he'd be gone.

How about life jackets. Did you have life jackets in the boat?
J - Oh, yeah. You had to, that was the rule.
C - I think that is what we used to learn how to swim. There was no beach there. Everything was deep.

Why did you swim mostly at the boathouse, not at the signal?
J - That was the best dock to swim.
C - Not only that, there was no supervision down there. (Laugh) Sometimes if we had a south wind, it would blow all that surface water out there and it would be warm. We'd go swimming some times three times a day.
J - Oh, was that nice.
C - We'd go out swimming, then back up to the house for something to eat, then back down and go swimming some more.

Do you remember the inspectors ever coming?
J - The only time I can remember the inspector coming was on that particular day that we had to keep the seagulls away.

C - Don't you remember when Dillon came there in 1936? We rode on the *Amaranth*.
J -Yeah.

You got a ride on that?
J - Yeah, they brought it into Skanee, into Huron Bay.
C - They brought it into Skanee.

Just for the fun of it?
J - No, no.
C - They had our furniture on there that they brought up from the Soo.

Did they off load the furniture in Skanee?
J - Yes.
C - Skanee.
J - The furniture they had on the island was something different than what we had at home.
C - This furniture was from the Soo for the house.

Did you have a car in Skanee?
C - Yeah, we had a Model A.

The Model A he bought with his fish money?
C - Yeah, right. We should have called it the herring car.

Looking at photo with Maude.
C - Old Maude, she was quite an old dandy, that old women.

Was she good to you kids?
C - Yes, she was.
J - They were both good natured. They were a good couple. I liked them. I liked the way he used to laugh with that cigarette holder hanging out of his mouth.

I guess all of them smoked?
J - Yes, dad smoked. Campbell smoked. Everybody smoked in those days.
C - Even you were smoking.
J - Yes, I was on the boat one time coming out from Skanee. I was 16 or 17. Dad offered me a cigarette. He said, "Here. I know you're doing it. You might as well smoke it." So I lit up and took about three or four puffs and I pinched it out and stuck it in my pocket for later.

Did they ever have any alcohol out there?
J - No. John Campbell was allowed. He's Native American and he could have one bottle a month, was it?
C - I didn't keep track of it.

Because he was Native American he was allowed?
J - Yes. And he was a World War I veteran. He was my hero.

He was your hero? Because he was a veteran?
J - He had bullet holes all over him. Five bullets. He was shot five times in World War I. So I took him as a hero.

But your dad also was a veteran.
J -Yes, but he never got overseas. He was in the army. Didn't he used to say he was a cook?
C - I think so, or a baker.
J - Baker.

That probably got him some preference in the lighthouse service.
J - Yes, being a veteran.
C - There were a lot of lighthouses at that time.
J - Yeah.

There is a line, see her holding on to it.?
C - That's the clothes line. This is a clothes line out front. Here is a clothes line pole.

Were there any antennae lines around?
C - This over here, in the back, was.

How were they hooked into the rock?
C - They weren't. That one was.

This was your sister Laurel. This is a wood sidewalk?
C - No, that was cement, a cement bridge.
J - There is a real long bridge there.
C - That goes over a gully like there. I think there were 63 or 64 steps from here up. It goes here, and then up to the left there, and around.

That was cement when you were kids?
C - Yes.

I understand that is still in pretty good shape.

C - Oh, yeah.

J - That's rebuilt, some of it. A tree fell down and broke the hand railing.

C - It didn't break the sidewalk, just the hand railing, that's all.

J - The organization replaced the hand railings.

C - What amazes me about those islands like that is that there is not a heck of a lot of dirt out there. How did that vegetation survive in July and August when the sun was so hot? The rocks get hot. How do they survive? Where do they get their moisture from?

J - There is one thing they did have out there was moss. If you got into it, it was really spongy. I assume this is where some of the moisture comes from for the trees. Also the tree roots go into the rocks. You have a big boulder and a tree on top and its roots are down the sides of the rock. Where can they get moisture on the side of a rock?

J - Lots of fog. Spring and fall.

C - When it gets hot like that, and those rocks get hot, you can take some of that vegetation and you can lift it up underneath, just like a rug, and that plant is still green. It is amazing what God can do.

What is this building?

C - That is the paint locker. That's the privy. I've got a good picture of that. That was a big one. It had four holes I think.

J - Brick. There is an expression, "Boy she's built like a brick outhouse." Well that's the brick outhouse. Who would want a women that looked like that?

Laurel Collins on the walk to the house from the boat house

Was this building here when you were there?
C - No, the Coast Guard put that up. I can't remember what year it was. They put that up for residential purposes, and they shut down the buildings up on top. That way, it was easier to get to the fog signal.

Do you remember that boat? What did you use that boat for?
C -That's for going to Skanee. That was built by a commercial fisherman up in Portage Entry. Winka Bros. built that in 1938, I think.

Was that a good boat?
J - It was like a cork.
C - Rocking and rolling, if you got into some heavy seas.
J - It was a lot of fun.

Did it have a name?
C - Nope.
J - It just had a number.

How long was it?
J - Eighteen or twenty feet. Four cylinder in it.

Can you swim that far?
C - Not me. I remember at one time there was a whole bunch of them left the dock there, swimming over to that island there. They had inner tubes, life preservers, everything they had to hang onto. I stayed on the dock. I wasn't ready yet. Campbell, Jim, my sisters.
J - Then, from Cattle Island we headed for Nelson Island, a mile away. With life preservers that's . . . got half way over and the water was just too cold for me. I went back. I don't know how much time I spent swimming. I was tired.
C - You were cuckoo. You must have been eating some fermented choke cherries.
C - Yes, there is a grape vine out there. It has got to be an old grape vine because it was there and well established in 1935.

Did your dad make more soda pop there?
C - No. Ma was starting to get a little religious at that time. She changed his mind on a few things. He didn't have much to say some times. She was quite a domi-nate woman. A good woman, but German dominate.
C - Yep, I wish my dad was alive today so I could thank him for that. Those islands . . . (tears)
J - Yes.

I would say that was true for the Campbells too. It was a special time of their lives.
J - Us too. Even the early part of my life that had been at Iroquois. . . I've been back there, I don't know how many times, and there are several memories. I have some pictures but I don't know where they are.

C - Huron Island was more special because dad was there for 18 years.

C - And actually, it was at an important time of our young lives.

C - That being out there taught us so many things. It taught us how to handle a boat, weather wise. All kinds of things that you don't get a chance otherwise, living in a city.

Jim and Clayton Collins during the interview

Detroit River Light

Boilers were very popular in the lighthouse service to make steam. In the days when wood was plentiful boilers could produce steam by burning wood, coal or oil. Steam, it was found could not only heat the lighthouse comfortably thru the use of radiators in the various rooms, but could also be used to blow the fog horns. In some lighthouses the boilers were housed in separate buildings away from the light and many contained two boilers, one to generate steam quickly and an additional one for sustained usage. In the first one the tubes, thru which the water passed, were thinner (of smaller wall sections) so the water heated quickly. These required more replacements and attention because if tubes leaked they put out the fire!

The Detroit River Light in Lake Erie was equipped with a unique use for steam.

Offshore lighthouses have always had challenging problems. One problem was, and continues to be, how to collect drinking water and what to do with sewage when finished. The solution: We drink the water from this side of the crib and we dump our sewage on the other side. That is how it was. When you look at original plans for crib lights you see the two pipes going out the opposite sides of the crib, one for water intake; one for sewage discharge.

The Detroit River Light was one of the first lights to have an inside water closet or toilet. It was in the boiler house, not in the light, and sewage was discharged thru a pipe into Lake Erie. In the early spring or late fall the stuff froze in the discharge pipe and clogged it. Here comes the inventor, he plumbs a steam line from the boiler to the toilet. In the early spring when ice may be present, you give the pipe a shot of high pressure steam to be sure the line is clear . . . . then you go! No more clogs!

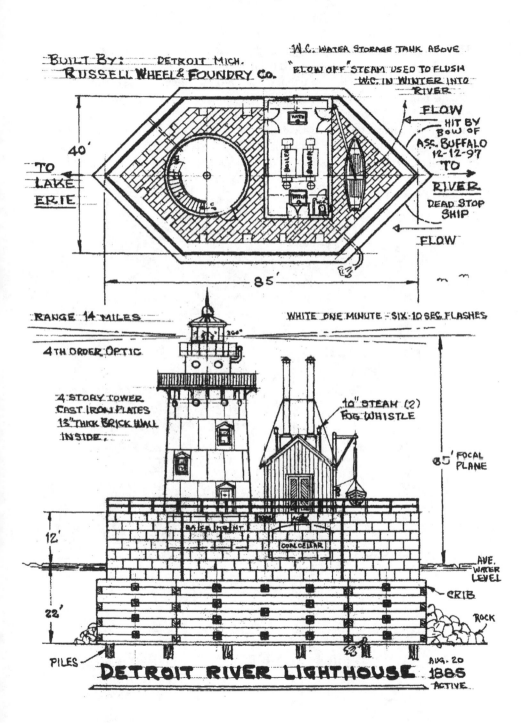

BUILT BY: DETROIT MICH.
RUSSELL WHEEL & FOUNDRY Co.

W.C. WATER STORAGE TANK ABOVE
"BLOW OFF" STEAM USED TO FLUSH
W.C. IN WINTER INTO
RIVER

FLOW
HIT BY
BOW OF
ASC. BUFFALO
12-12-97
TO
RIVER
DEAD STOP
SHIP

FLOW

40'

TO
LAKE
ERIE

85'

RANGE 14 MILES

WHITE ONE MINUTE - SIX 10 SEC. FLASHES

4TH ORDER OPTIC

4 STORY TOWER
CAST IRON PLATES
13" THICK BRICK WALL
INSIDE.

10" STEAM (2)
FOG WHISTLE

85' FOCAL
PLANE

BAILER INCINT

COAL CELLAR

12'

AVE.
WATER
LEVEL

CRIB

ROCK

22'

PILES

DETROIT RIVER LIGHTHOUSE

AUG. 20
1885
ACTIVE

The Detroit River Light had a large cavernous coal cellar built into the lighthouse base. The coal was conveyor loaded from a boat into a chute and gravity pulled it down into the coal cellar. Getting the coal into the cellar was easy but getting it into the boiler to burn was another story. Someone had to crawl down into the coal pile and fill a pail that was dropped down from above. The pail was then pulled to the boiler room and unloaded. Coal was always kept on hand in the boiler house, but when it ran out more had to be hand lifted from the cellar. All this work in addition to carrying 5-gallon cans of kerosene up the steps daily to fuel the light!

- Heinz Wernecke

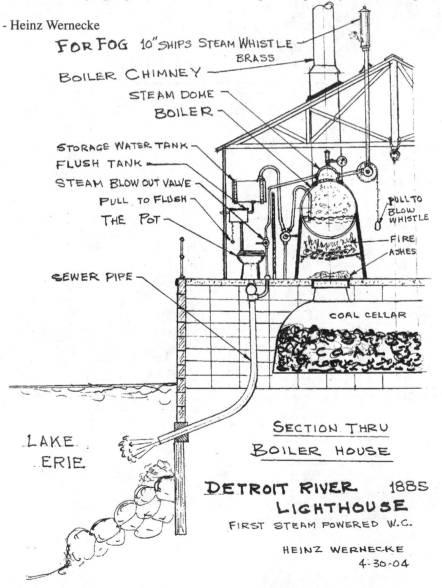

FOR FOG 10" SHIPS STEAM WHISTLE
BRASS
BOILER CHIMNEY
STEAM DOME
BOILER
STORAGE WATER TANK
FLUSH TANK
STEAM BLOW OUT VALVE
PULL TO FLUSH
THE POT
PULL TO BLOW WHISTLE
FIRE
ASHES
SEWER PIPE
COAL CELLAR
COAL
LAKE ERIE

SECTION THRU
BOILER HOUSE

DETROIT RIVER 1885
LIGHTHOUSE
FIRST STEAM POWERED W.C.

HEINZ WERNECKE
4-30-04

6

William Simon

Served from 1956 to 1958

Interviewed September 15, 2003 by Terry Pepper by email

Bill Simon was one of the young Coast Guard kids that the old keepers talked about with dismay. What was the lighthouse service coming to? These young, inexperienced, homesick kids were sent to isolated stations without the skills to be productive.

Bill was just such a "coastie." At 19 years old and single, he was care-free. He joined up to have an adventure. And he did have that adventure, but not the high action adventure that he saw on television. He was stationed on isolated Martin Reef Light.

As a seaman, the lowest rank, he worked with three other more experienced men. Hence he was assigned the routine, non-skilled work like painting. He got along, did not get homesick, and enjoyed the life. But you can sense that at 19 he did not yet understand the serious role he was stepping into.

He remembers two sobering events. The first was being left alone at the station for five days during a heavy fog. Although everything went smoothly, he knew he did not have the necessary skills if any of the equipment malfunctioned. The second was trying to return to the lighthouse in fog in a very small boat traveling through the shipping channel. It was a life threatening position and he was lucky to survive. These two serious occasions clouded the otherwise sunny times.

Bill did not remain with the service. The isolation and danger were not compatible with the family life he had in mind. Yet forty years later, he feels he would enjoy returning to Martin Reef and the quiet solitary life.

Richard L. Moehl

Martin Reef Light in northern Lake Huron

Bill Simon

Bill Simon standing on the ice covered deck of Martin Reef Light

Where did you grow up, and how did you come to be in the Coast Guard?
I grew up in Milwaukee, Wisconsin. One day I was watching TV and saw this neat commercial for the Coast Guard showing a Coast Guard boat going through the rough weather, and then some Coast Guardsman climbing aboard a ship to make an inspection. Looked like the type of thing for me. While in high school I joined the Coast Guard Reserves and about a year later went active. The year was 1955. My first duty station was the Coast Guard Cutter *Mesquite* (W-305) buoy tender, at that time out of Sault Ste. Marie, Michigan. This ship went aground about two or three years ago, was de-commissioned and was sunk.

How did you get out to the station at the opening of navigation?
The first year was by the Coast Guard Cutter *Woodbine*. It took us out because of heavy ice. The second year it was the *Mesquite*. In both cases, they brought us to within about 300 to 400 yards of the light. The rest of the way was via a barge.

Do you have any recollections of opening the station at the beginning of the navigation season, and what was the routine for opening-up?
No set routine. First was to chop ice off the rungs leading up the side of the crib so we could get onboard. This took a little time as each rung had to be cleared to go to the next step. Once at the top it was dangerous going due to the ice. The barge left with the cutter but returned hours later to deliver our supplies. We went about the task of chopping ice at the entrance to get in during that time. Once in, the first thing that was done was to get lights and heat. The generators and air compressors were serviced and powered up. It was very cold and damp in the station and the heat was very welcomed. After that we went about settling in. When the ship returned, we were somewhat ready to take supplies aboard. There would still be a lot of ice outside, and it would be hard to walk and stand.

How was the "dungeon" set up, and what type of equipment was located there?
I did not spend much time down in the "dungeon" so I don't really recall it too much. There were about two or three rooms with steel doors. I was told that at one time one room was a "coal bin." Now it was used as a paint locker. We also stored other flammable materials in there. Diesel fuel was also stored in the dungeon. Diesel was our source of fuel for the generators and compressors. We cooked by propane gas that was outside the main part of the light.

Bill Simon

A chair and the deck covered with ice

How were the upper floors laid out?
As you walked in through the entrance, the first or main floor housed two generators and two air compressors, a large hot water tank and lots of pipes. The stairs
were off to the left, and under those going up were the steps to the dungeon going
down. The second floor had the galley, office, storage room and TV room. On the
third floor were the bedrooms, bathroom (no shower just a tub) and radio room.
The next floor was the tower (light room and the light itself.)

Do you recollect the color scheme inside the station?
Easy....... White, gray and pea green

*Was it comfortably warm in the lighthouse during the cold early spring and late
fall?*
Yes, we were always nice and warm. We did not have to pay any heating bills, so
we had the temperature turned up to keep us as warm as we wanted. With the wind
coming through the windows sometimes we had it turned up high.

*Access to the "dungeon" basement was by a step ladder. Notice the
jacket with Martin Reef embroidered on the back*

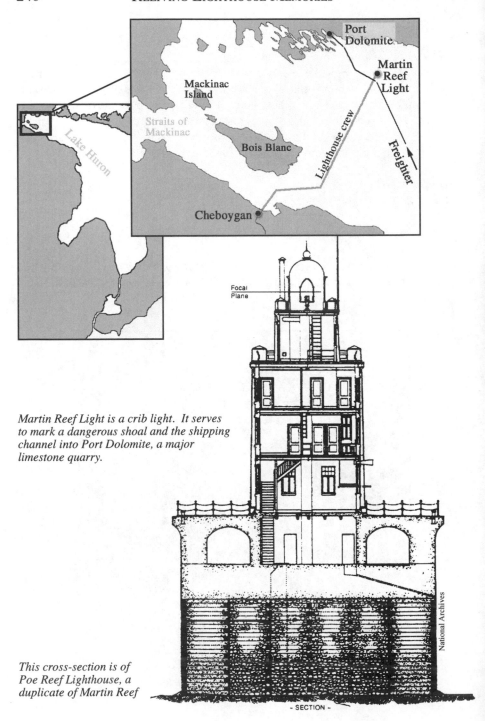

Martin Reef Light is a crib light. It serves to mark a dangerous shoal and the shipping channel into Port Dolomite, a major limestone quarry.

This cross-section is of Poe Reef Lighthouse, a duplicate of Martin Reef

How many seamen were assigned to the station and what were your scheduled watches?
There were four men assigned to the station:

      one 1st class petty officer (engineer) also officer in charge,
      one 2nd class boatswain's mate (second in command),
      one 3rd class engineer, and
      one seaman (me).

We really did not have a formal schedule for watches. It seemed like it just worked itself out as needed. Someone couldn't sleep, they stayed up and watched TV. Someone was ALMOST awake all the time. On a clear and star-filled sky we never were too concerned. For the record, we had a scheduled watch. Someone was up and down all night long looking at the weather.

Could you describe a typical day at the station?
We generally did routine maintenance. Clean and mop the floors as needed. Wash windows and, in general, keep the place clean. After all, this was our home. We painted the station in and out in the two years I was on Martin Reef. Hanging above the crib in a boatswain's chair was a little scary, but I got used to it. Most of the time the two engineers were stripping down and repairing the compressors or

Bill Simon

This photo, showing Bill at work in an office, tells you as much about the times as about the lighthouse. The old typewriter, telephone, and even the desk are from another era.

generators. When they could, they would help with the painting. We almost always stopped work after lunch unless we were into something big that needed to get finished.

Did you have to radio-in at any specific times during the day?
Yes, twice a day was required. We were in radio contact with the Coast Guard Group Office in Cheboygan at 11 a.m. and 4 p.m. Otherwise the radio was NOT on. Our call signs were NMP-18 (funny how you remember something like that).

What type of radio equipment was on board?
I did not know much about the radio except how to use it. What kind it was, no idea. The only other "radio equipment" we had was a TV and a regular type radio.

One of your photos shows you talking on what appears to be a telephone handset. Were you able to radiotelephone to family?
The telephone headset you see was one of two ways to hear and talk. We could go manual on speakers, or on the headset. The headset was easier and better to hear with. It was used only for radio communication between Coast Guard units. No other calls were made or, to my knowledge, could be made. We were able to talk to other lights (Poe Reef and Spectacle Reef) if we would go on line when their assigned time was. The only unit that we could reach in the event of an emergency would be the Mackinac Island CG Station (now the Mackinac State Historic Parks Welcome Center).

If you were allowed to radiotelephone to family, how frequently, and for how long?
No, we were unable to call out other than as stated above.

How frequently did you go to shore to get food?
When one of us was scheduled to go on liberty, then the person taking him would return with supplies, food and mail. This was about twice a month. Once in a great while we would sneak a trip into

The telephone receiver was connected to the large box.

Cedarville and take a few hours of R&R and bring back some beer. When the Group Commander would come out for his monthly inspection he would bring us mail, etc. and that's when we would "hang our beer by a rope over the side of the crib." No beer was permitted on the light. Some rules are meant to be broken. It was something we did not abuse. The CO (Commanding Officer) would come out from Mackinac Island via the 40-footer, and we would see him coming for miles away.

Which cutter(s) or buoy tenders serviced the station? How frequently did they come to the station?
The Coast Guard Cutter *Mesquite* and the Cutter *Woodbine*. Once a year.

Living quarters were close and sparse

How close could such large vessels get to the crib? How were things transferred to the main lighthouse deck?
About 300 to 400 yards off to the west of the light. Bring them in close via a barge, then be lifted on the crib by the crane.

How did the crane operate by steam, diesel, electric, etc. ?
Best I can recall, it was by electric power.

Do you have any interesting recollections about operating the crane?
The crane was very reliable and well maintained.

The "liberty" boat. Notice how it hangs from a sling with an eye. The crane had a hook.

Every Coast Guard person stationed on an island has fond memories of their "liberty."

Bill Simon

How about raising and lowering the liberty boat - do you remember any close calls or humorous moments in doing so?
This was sometimes a real challenge. It had to be timed just right. The crane had a big hook on it and the lighthouse boat had a sling with an eye on it. When a swell lifted the boat up, you had to be ready to put the hook in the eye. If you missed, you would go with the swell and hit the side of the crib. If you made it, the boat would be out of the water for a few seconds as the swell flowed away. At the same time the crane operator had to be lifting you up. It did not matter how hard the surf was blowing, it all was a matter of timing. It was very difficult if only one man was on the boat. This happened a few times if one person was returning after leaving one man on shore.

You had to get the boat in the right position, go outside and grab the hook and place it in the eye, and be ready to go back inside the boat to operate it if you missed. This could be touch and go. Sometimes, when you left Cheboygan it was calm and the weather good. By the time you reached the light, things could have gotten a little rough. It was about 2-3/4 hours from Cheboygan to the light via the 25-foot boat.

What parts of the station were the crew responsible for painting?
As mentioned earlier, we took care of everything.

Was any of the painting sub-contracted?
No.

Bill Simon

It was a good life. Notice the pin-up of Kim Novak and the Strohs.

Exactly what was done to the station and systems to prepare for winter?
We left no perishable food behind, nothing that could freeze. When we left the station for good, our boat was loaded with paint and all other supplies. We secured all windows and sealed them the best we could. We put antifreeze in the toilet and pipes, winterized the generators and air compressors, pulled down all storm shutters and simply closed up for the winter.

Could you tell me more about the time you were "marooned" at the station while the other crewmen were in Cheboygan for five days?
We always tried to send two men with the boat at all times. When the boat left the station it was because one man was going on liberty, and the other would be taking him in. He would pick up supplies and return after gassing up. This day was clear and calm. The officer in charge took the 3rd class in for liberty, expecting to return within hours. After he went grocery shopping in town, the weather turned very bad. The Group Commander would not allow him out by himself for safety reasons. We got high wind, swells and rain. Out at the light the waves were 10 to 12 feet with a driving rain and fog. For five days this went on. I kept our radio on all the time, but there was nothing more I could do except watch the weather and turn

Bill Simon

If you look closely at this photo of Martin Reef Light, you will see arrows pointing to Bill Simon's bedroom. It is also the place that he woke up one morning to find about an inch of water on the floor from waves breaking in the window during the storm that night.

the fog horn on if needed. I was 19 years old, and I was scared stiff. One night I heard a ship blowing its horn in the dark, and he sounded to me like he was right outside my door. Our horn was blowing and the sea was hitting the side of the crib, making a sound like a big base drum. I couldn't sleep if I wanted to. I catnapped during the day. I thought, "What would happen if the compressors or generators failed, what would I do?" We had back-up for both, but they were being overhauled at the time. But I made it OK. I was really happy when I looked through the glasses and saw our boat returning. I will never forget those five days.

The brass work in the lens photo looks well polished - how frequently did the crew clean the lens?
We polished the brass and lens daily.

What did you or the other crew members do in your "spare time" on station?
At night we watched TV, played cards, read and wrote letters and listened to the radio. On nice days we lowered the skiff, tied a long rope to it and let it drift away while we fished and just sun bathed. We never caught anything.

How were cooking duties handled, and what type of meals were most hated and enjoyed?

Bill Simon

We always ate good. Each one of us received a special allowance for food. What we spent was up to us. We would shop for whatever we wanted then split the bill four ways. We always had extra money to save for our liberty. We ate like kings. Steak or whatever we wanted. Cooking? Whoever felt like it. If you could cook something special - do it. Never had any problems finding someone who wanted to cook. The cook didn't have to do dishes. We baked pies, made cakes and just about anything.

Did you ever have any civilian visitors out at the station?
We were in the shipping lanes for pleasure boats going from The Islands to the St. Marys River. Nine out of 10 boats would stop. Sometimes they would come up the side of the crib and visit us, or we

would go down to their boat. They would always offer us a cold beer, and we would never say no. They found our life very interesting.

Did you have any close calls, either at the station or traveling back and forth on the liberty boat?
This one time, the situation changed. The OIC (Officer In Charge) and I were on shore. He had come in to pick up supplies and me, as I was returning from liberty. One man, again, was out on the light, this time it wasn't me. The weather was going bad but, because there were two of us, the Group Commander OK'd us leaving for the light. All we had on the 25-foot boat was a compass, life preservers, a horn and fire extinguisher, no radios. About half way to the light the weather really got bad. A lot of fog. Couldn't see more than five feet in any direction. We started to hear the "thump, thump" of the turning screws of a freighter. We knew he was close. We turned off the engine to try and figure out which way he was going. He let out a loud blow of his horn. Now we knew he was close. I'm sure he had us on his radar, but we had no idea where he was. We started back up and were going again for about five minutes, when right in front of us passed this huge wall. It was the freighter, not far away, in fact, right in front of us. As he went by, all we heard was the water splashing and the thump, thump of his screws. For me, much too close. We made it to the light and I, for one, was sure glad to be "home".

Do you remember anything particularly humorous during your time at the station?
One time this pleasure boat stopped and came up to the light. This very big, heavy women climbed up the side of the crib. How she did it I still don't know. At any rate, after they decided to leave she couldn't go down. This guy got under her (she had a sun dress on) and tried to ease her down, but that didn't work. Well, to make a long story short, we ended up rigging a boatswain's chair for her and lowering her down with the crane. You probably could hear her screaming all the way to Cheboygan, along with our laughter.

Bill Simon

Bill Simon today.

Did you have much trouble with gulls at the station? How about bugs and spiders?
We caught this seagull once while fishing. We painted its wings green and black. He (she) was around all summer and we named it "Hobart." Droppings were a common thing, and we tried to keep ahead of that. Some spiders and flies, but not many.

What is your fondest memory of your time at Martin Reef?
Just being able to experience all that I've talked about. Martin Reef really got to be home.

What is your worst memory about your time at the station?
None.

Did you serve at any other light stations, or on any of the cutters or buoy tenders on the Great Lakes?
I had TAD (temporary additional duty) for six months at Old Mackinac Point Light station from March to May of 1956, two weeks at Cheboygan Group Office (River Range Light) in March of 1956, a couple of short stays at Poe and Spectacle Reef, a short stay on the *Mackinaw* and the Coast Guard Cutter *Mesquite*, and TAD at six lights in Door County, Wisconsin and Wind Point, Wisconsin.

My winters were at Traverse City Air Station, Traverse City, Mich. (TAD) That is also the time they allowed us to take regular leave. Because I was TAD, I could take 30 days leave over the holidays and some of my compensatory leave.

When did you leave the Coast Guard and why did you decide to leave?
I left the Coast Guard in 1963. My wife at that time wanted her own home and wanted me out of the Coast Guard. I chose my family.

What do you remember about the Cheboygan River Front Range Light?
My first and only TAD at Cheboygan River Range Light was while waiting to be sent out to Martins Reef. This is the best that I can recall, as most of the time I was working outside or doing other things.

Cheboygan River Range Light was then also called the Cheboygan Group Office. The CO was Henry V. Devereaux, CHBOSN W-2. The Group Office had under its command all of the lights and lifeboat stations in the area. (This also included Mackinac Island Lifeboat Station.) I'm not sure if the CO had any CG personnel assigned with him, but I do think there was one. He did have a civilian keeper working with him. The keeper's name, as I recall, was Clarence Land. He and his family lived upstairs. The CO and his family had a place in town.

As the Group Office, it was our source of orders and supplies (for the lights). It also was our "jumping off" point. We would tie up our boats at the dock for however long it would take to go into town and purchase groceries etc. and drop off and pick up members of the crew that would be on leave. Also this was where our mail was sent. This is also the station that we were in radio contact with on Martins Reef. In most cases, one or two 25-footers from the lights would be tied up at one time. Now and then the 40-footer from Mackinac Island would be tied up as well. So, this office was HQ for the lights in the area. This also was the CO that made monthly inspections of the lights.

The inside of the building was painted CG green and white. The best I recall there were three or four offices in use. The back one was the CO's office, one was for the radio, the main one, as you walked in the door, was just that, the main office area. I think there was a bathroom on the right in the back. I was never in the civilian quarters, but I was up in the tower maybe twice. Just to the south of the station we would park our cars while on the lights. They were watched by the civilian keeper.

While on TAD I did meet this girl who was a senior in high school. She went to school on the east side of the Cheboygan bridge and lived on the west side. So she would cross the bridge each day going home. When our boat was in I would hang a white rag on the end (bow) of our boat. When she saw that she would know I was in. As it turned out I married her two years after we met, so now I have two daughters and two sons still living in the Cheboygan area, and, my now ex-wife. So I know Cheboygan fairly well.

Did you learn anything in your time at Martin Reef which has stuck with you through your life?
You can make what you want of any situation. If you are afraid to try something new, you will never have any good experiences. I enjoyed the lights very much. Would I do it all over again? Without even thinking about it. I'd love to live on a light now. It's an experience you never forget.

Cheboygan River Front Range Light

Sandra L. Planisek

Epilogue

Reliving lighthouse memories was a joyful experience for the interviewers and interviewees. We got to know these people and enjoyed talking to each and every one. But is there more here than seven stories?

What has been the effect of these people and their service? Would today's world be any different if they had not performed this duty? Good lighthouse keeping relieved a lot of mariner anxiety and kept some ships safe that otherwise might not have been safe. Making an industry safe facilitates its continuance. Had light-house keepers not succeeded perhaps all shipping today would be done by rail and truck transportation. But no, ships today are bigger and faster than ever.

On another level, lighthouse keepers have grown into today's heroes. This is an interesting phenomena. Former heroes such as presidents, inventors, and soldiers were public figures. But modern cynicism has investigated, analyzed and criti-cized the heroism out of these leaders. Former heroes have been de-throned. Light-house keepers, on the other hand, were reclusive figures that will be extremely difficult to de-throne because of the scarcity of information about them as indi-viduals. They will live and survive as role models as a group. Perhaps this is ideal for our age. The job of lighthouse keeper was not designed to be a heroic job but perhaps this heroic legacy is even more important to society than safe shipping.

Who were these people? They were people who fell into this job that launched them into fame. Remember that we interviewed only those who did not quit the lighthouse service. Thus we met people capable of surviving in isolated locations, under a regimented lifestyle with repetitive work. This is certainly a select sub-set of people. They were more followers than leaders, yet they did take the initiative when necessary. They had to be adaptable.

This leads to the next interesting question. If we were looking for similar people today where would we look? These would have to be people who serve mankind in their profession, they would live in isolated and poorly understood conditions, they would battle nature not their fellow men, and they would be anonymous, receiving no special pay or notoriety as they work. What set of workers meet this criteria today? Who will tomorrow's heroes be?

Were the lighthouse keepers truly unique?

Next

This is the second of GLLKA's oral history books. These books are written to fulfill a portion of our mission statement. The former keepers are getting old and thus GLLKA is collecting these histories at a faster pace. GLLKA has a third oral history book in process. It, too, will include a range of people from an assortment of lighthouses who performed varied tasks. The following pages give a hint of the life of John Tregembo, one of the keepers in the next book.

What was your position?
Bottom of the ladder I guess, seaman first class In the olden days you used to show your rank on your uniform. There were three stripes. When you were apprentice seaman there was one stripe. When you made seaman second class you got two stripes. When you got to be seaman first class you got to wear three stripes. Then you got to wear the white band on your uniform and, if you were in the black gang, engineering, you wore a red band on that arm.

What was your first impression?
I went out there in a mail boat from Grand Marais, Minnesota in about May. They called it the pickle boat, from Detroit. They used to make the trip from Grand Marais, go all the way around Isle Royale, stop at all the fishermen places, pick up fish, bring it back to Grand Marais, then they would bring the fish down to Duluth. This boat was about 65-foot long. We went into Washington Harbor to unload our supplies. We had a 25-foot lighthouse boat with a four cylinder engine that would be waiting. Single screw. It had a cabin. That is how we got from Washington Harbor to Rock of Ages.

When you came into the dock at Rock of Ages there was only one man in the boat. I didn't know how to run a boat so they had sent a man with the boat to get me. When they came into the dock they had a yolk on there with a big ring. They had the boom down. As soon as you got near the dock you'd cut the engine and throw it in reverse. You would run out and hook the boom onto that ring and they'd lift you up out of the water.

One man did this?
One man did this in all kinds of weather.

How many times did you have to try before you caught the ring?
You only had one chance. There are four cables, you had to get outside the cabin and hook it on the ring. They would lift you up as soon as it was on there.

ROCK OF AGES LIGHT HOUSE, WASHINGTON HARBOR, ISLE ROYALE NATIONAL PARK

Terry Pepper

So you didn't tie up to the dock?
Very seldom. You learn how to do that. They lift it up out of the water. You would get out of the boat on the deck. You would have a whip, a small cable, you would pull the boom over there. Opposite the entrance you would store the boat. That's how we docked the boat. It was always stored up there in a cradle on the east side.

This mail boat came on a regular schedule?
Right. That is how you went on your compensatory absence.

Is that a government phrase for vacation, compensatory absence?
Right. You were out there 21 days. After 21 days you would go in town and do whatever you wanted to do for seven days.

Town was?
Grand Marais. That was the landing spot.

Who was at the light when you got there?
There was a first class bosun named Andy Anderson. There was another first class bosun mate named Bill Williamson, his dad was a lighthouse keeper around Whitefish Point, Crisp Point and the lighthouse in Grand Marais, Michigan. His dad had served around that area.

Watch the *Beacon* for the announcement of this publication date!

Index

258

Useful Web Sites

www.baconlibrary.org
http://photography-plus.com/lighthouses.htm
www.terrypepper.com
www.uscg.mil/hq/g-cp/history/weblighthouses/lhmi.html
www.gllka.com
www.michiganlights.com

GLLKA Publications

To order any GLLKA publication call 231-436-5580 or visit our web store at www.GLLKA.com

Books

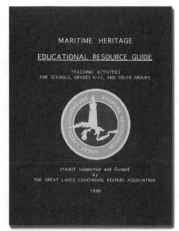

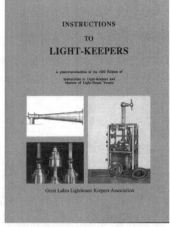

Educational Resource Guide 4th Edition
Contain 109 lesson plans and activities on the Great Lakes and their lighthouses with worksheets that can be copied for students. Covers Michigan benchmarks.
Softcover $17.00

Instructions to Lightkeepers
A photoreproduction of the 1902 edition of the original publication by the U. S. Lighthouse Establishment. See the actual list of duties, rules, diagrams of equipment. This was the official handbook.
Softcover $18.00   Hardcover $23.00

Travel map

Music

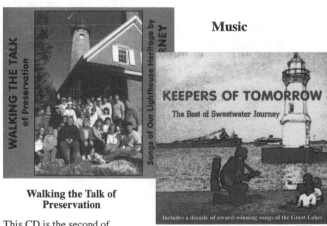

Walking the Talk of Preservation

This CD is the second of Sweetwater Journey's music donated to GLLKA for fund raising. It documents our struggles to perserve and pass on our lighthouse heritage.
$14.95

Keepers of Tomorrow
by Sweetwater Journey
Delightufl and upbeat songs with historical accuracy. 23 songs, 67 minutes $14.95

Handy glove-box map to help locate lighthouses anywhere on the Great Lakes. Makes planning easy. Each light is rated: lighthouse with keepers quarters, structure to hold a light, minor light, ruins, museum, not accessible, private aid to navigation, lightship.
$6.95